AF449349

Toward a Grammar
of Abstraction

Literature & Philosophy

A. J. Cascardi, General Editor

This new series will publish books in a wide range of subjects in philosophy and literature, including studies of the social and historical issues that relate these two fields. Drawing on the resources of the Anglo-American and Continental traditions, the series will be open to philosophically informed scholarship covering the entire range of contemporary critical thought.

Already published:

J. M. Bernstein, *The Fate of Art: Aesthetic Alienation from Kant to Derrida and Adorno*

Mary E. Finn, *Writing the Incommensurable: Kierkegaard, Rossetti, and Hopkins*

Peter Bürger, *The Decline of Modernism*

Toward a Grammar *of* Abstraction

MODERNITY, WITTGENSTEIN, *and* THE PAINTINGS *of* JACKSON POLLOCK

Robert Steiner

The Pennsylvania State University Press
University Park, Pennsylvania

The author and publisher are grateful to the Committee on University Scholarly Publishing of the University of Colorado for a subvention toward the publication of this book.

Library of Congress Cataloging-in-Publication Data

Steiner, Robert, 1948–
     Toward a grammar of abstraction: modernity, Wittgenstein, and the paintings of Jackson Pollock / Robert Steiner.
          p.   cm.
     Includes bibliographical references (p.   )
     ISBN 0-271-00866-0 (acid-free paper)
     1. Aesthetics.   2. Representation (Philosophy)   3. Pollock, Jackson, 1912–1956.   4. Wittgenstein, Ludwig, 1889–1951.
     I. Title.
     BH39.S8145   1992
     111'.85—dc20   92-6984
                                                                          CIP

Published by The Pennsylvania State University Press,
Suite C, Barbara Building, University Park, PA 16802-1003

Contents

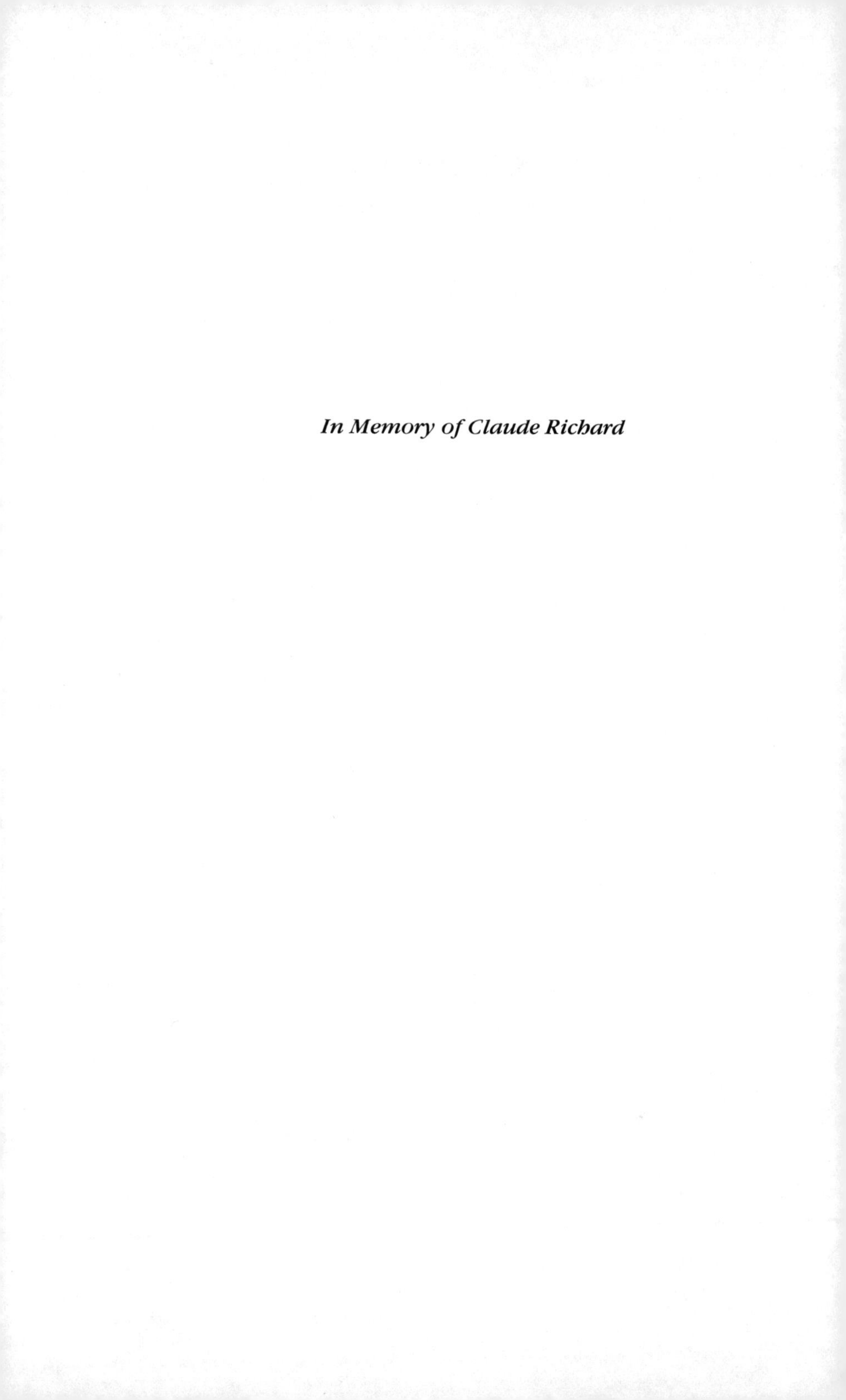

In Memory of Claude Richard

PROLOGUE
The Arc of Representation

It is characteristic of art studies, as it is of philosophy, that they must repeatedly confront the problem of representation. The historical relations between sacred image, nature and truth, distinct from any theoretical history of knowledge or ideas, persistently attempt to describe, explain or reconcile the distance between icon or image and an "authenticity" of artistic figuration. If philosophy tends toward doctrine or system, as the movement from medieval to modern suggests, it is no less so that the study of art relies upon a humanist paradigm whose authority, in its claims of representational truth, forgets that only knowledge can be possessed. The power of institutional thinking, structured by tradition, enables analysis to slip past philosophical doubt like sneakered felons on a moonless night. Such analysis presumes a resolution of the problem of the truth of art because by replacing philosophical rigor with rational methodology one can project an onto-theological dream of representation as if it were as authentic as daylight; in this regard positivist transparency and dialectical history are indistinguishable. As Benjamin noted in the *Trauerspiel,* "Knowledge is open to question, truth is not," a description accounting for the appetite of institutions of knowledge to make greater claims for the unity of understanding about their tasks. If there is agreement about an arrow flung from representation toward truth, the imp of unfriendly details and spontaneous fragmentation can be left like the trickster in Cassirer's accurately gloomy picture of totality in which heresy resides subsumed and explained in the grand untrue idea. In most thinking about the pictorial, *conceptual* unity concerning the phenomenal bases of art studies stands as if it were an essential unity of art, a truth whose appearance surpasses dubiety and whose means are no longer visible. In this scenario coherence and truth are confused, tradition and method conflated, and whatever fails to exist under the totalizing umbrella of, for example, art-historical aesthetics, abides as a digression as merely inconvenient as a sun shower. In that ancient mental space elsewise reserved for nostalgia and new physics, where truth must be beautiful, simultaneously and contradictorily stand cohesion and subjectivity like scales awaiting the sultan's birthday and his subjects' desultory contributions.

On the one hand, a problem persists within the realm of representation that traditionally unites the disparate features of art, philosophy and literature; on the other, details of overlain methodological trials remain at once distinct and muddy, and therefore vehemently hidden. Where both psychology and sociology have proven ham-handed in the study of literature, they have flourished in the study of art and been ignored in the practice of philosophy; while visual theory can vitalize a consideration of Vermeer and Velázquez, it offers little momentum to a discussion of Russellian pink rats in a corner or the actual color of Emma Bovary's eyes. Conceptual differences among discrete disciplines are irreconcilable; what motivates conjugal visitations between them is the status of discourse, whose problematic understanding of representation, truth and the authority of institutions impels contemporary theory. Here everyone speaks the same language, when they choose to speak at all. If meta-discourse is designed to reveal ideology, it presumably brings us nearer to the object by bringing the object nearer to our cultural need of it. However, it remains unconvincing to suggest that this is the crux of the matter, that, for example, subject-object relations are necessarily dialectical, or that claims of the "open work," sweeping panoramically among the greatest number of needs and interests, can inform us better about the meaning of objects themselves or, more urgently, the meaning of our relationship to them. The valorization of intersubjective relations, whether represented by versions of dialectic or, contrarily, etymologically inspired disseminating codes, does not ensure the meaningfulness of interdisciplinary practice; often one uncovers the displacement of rules of representation by rules of nonrepresentation or a void the former rules demark by their violation. Even the most radical theories of knowledge inchoately establish relational models as if culture either replaced or originated in a natural language so that even in, for example, the extreme case of de Man, rhetoric can be treated as an allegory of illusory natural relations. Bringing the self-consciousness of language to the fore does not itself assure us of understanding language better; rather, we understand the self-consciousness of representational thinking which, unless it substitutes for metaphysics, is an attribute of philosophical or even Burkean grammar and not an object of study. In short, the immanent criticism of meta-discourse does not escape its own methodological frangibility.

The category representation/nonrepresentation lingers as primitive residue not only from a genealogy originating in sacred image but from a tradition whose precepts venture to explain nature, culture and concepts of realism as qualitatively interchangeable. The primary function of the category has been to bridge an abyss between "untranslatable" art and the dream of truth the beauty of art signifies; in brief, representation thematizes the problem between art and its linguistic analysis, providing an ostensive object of study where otherwise there might be silence. Saying that representation provides the foundation of a sentimental aesthetic whose metaphysical yearning reads like false mystery is to suggest that whether present, absent or illusory, representation as a category has featured in the systematic coercions whereby psychology, theories of perception, and cultural critique offer vocabularies presumed to interpret the abstractions of art. Because representation stands for the problem of mediation in art, mediation (translatability) can be brushed aside; to this extent, representation has become a shaggy-dog story in which, as in myth, the sacred and profane elements exist in bedridden indifference rump to rump. The rhetoric of representation disguises the dead thought of metaphysics that adheres to statements about the meaning of art, turning contingent spatial relations into necessary linguistic ones, thereby to demonstrate that paintings, for example, are not only semantic mysteries but *prima facie* universal ones. This is the institutional fetish that across disciplines representation has become.

Within disciplines the variant features of genres, subgenres and uncollectible oddities confess the paradoxical status and insufficient understanding of the problem of representation to the point where "representation of representation" (e.g., Lichtenstein's painting of Loran's diagram of Cézanne's portrait of Madame Cézanne) remains tethered to a concept of truth at once as authoritative, subjective and ephemeral as Cézanne's original—and here one might digress without sacrifice to Picasso's portrait of Gertrude Stein, which imitates the Cézanne. The "indistinction" of identifying by quotation, once it has been appropriately accounted for in tradition, seems to have no bearing on the fundamental truth content of a work of art; rather, the content of the concept of truth merely enlarges. Were this not so, radical dislocations (among them, self-consuming parodies) would demand a rethinking of originary aesthethics rather than a self-comprehending notion of artistic "development." If the pedagogical aspect of art analysis distinguished between knowledge, representation and truth in such a way that genre became no more than an archival tool, albeit misleading, any notion of a moveable tradition based on anything other than stated influence would be meaningless. And what precisely would the study of art contain but gratuitous categories of random examples zealously collated by earnest viewers hoping to make a synthesis of artistic whim? As a result broad contentious visual theories, delineated by psychological, cultural or transcendental forms, rest categorically distinct from hoary archival notations but nonetheless totalized within institutional practices that assume truth, knowledge and representation to be not only compatible but necessarily present.

In literature the famous case of Frenhofer's *Catherine* signals the unwritten history of this distress. At the climax of Balzac's "Unknown Masterpiece" the youthful Poussin, "returning to his position before the alleged painting," can discern "nothing but colors piled upon one another in confusion," only to be informed by the older Porbus that "standing out from that colorful chaos, the uncertain tones of that shapeless mist, is a lovely foot, a living foot!" The recognition that "there is a woman underneath" does not of course diminish the catastrophe the painting is judged to be because it corresponds to nothing in Poussin's understanding of art, let alone of "masterpiece." That Frenhofer dies later that night after burning his work only adds credence to the distance between the *Catherine* and Frenhofer's Louis Lambertian idealization, "marking the end of art on earth." While we know that Balzac does not intend us to view Frenhofer as simply an atrocious painter not worth our attention, the ambiguous attribution of "madman" to him is less in doubt because Poussin, throughout the career we know he will later have, in reality borrows nothing from Frenhofer's example. How, in light of Poussin's genius (and Balzac's choice of him as spectator), are we then to read Frenhofer, or for that matter vice versa? Within the tale we know what the painting signifies, but the matter muddies if we add Poussin's work to the reading, and of course doubly so by drawing both into Balzac's world. The interpretation of a Catherine tradition, the portraiture of the mistress Gillette and the grander aesthetic ideal marking the route of Frenhofer's career, do not amount in Balzac's story to a statement on his part of avant-garde genius. Later, Cézanne will consciously adopt the Frenhofer persona to rationalize his own marginality (according to Bernard's memoir) and, arguably, eventually de Kooning will commence his "Woman" series so that the Frenhofer *Catherine* can "remind" us of de Kooning—notably, had Meyer Shapiro not salvaged the first of de Kooning's "women," pronouncing it finished and successful rather than, as de Kooning had decided, unfinished and impossible, neither it nor its successors would necessarily be there to remind us of anything. Within the Balzac tale Frenhofer's problem is not a lack of talent nor of imagination; it is a problem of representation rather than truth if, indeed, we accept the master's reputation as an indicator. It gradually becomes a problem of audience when artists from Cézanne and Gauguin to Picasso view Frenhofer as a heroic model, and in so doing encourage art studies to focus greater attention on the figure of the artist in society; none of them in fact imitates or quotes the *Catherine* itself, thereby drawing us away from the painted object to, for example, the suffering of Van Gogh, the exile of Gauguin, the derision of Cézanne. Historically, then, and within theories of art for a century, while the figure of Frenhofer had psychological and cultural significance, as well as aesthetic metaphorical value, his masterpiece did not, remaining for all intents and purposes the assiduously described cautionary example not only of the distances between real and ideal, consumer and producer, but of representation and truth. In a sense the vocabularies of painting and reading could not accommodate the object itself toward the "disinterested intentionlessness of truth," as Benjamin characterized the latter.

Reiterating the primacy of artist over object, Henry James's "Madonna of the Future" consciously takes the Balzac tale one step further. Whereas Frenhofer paints a "chaos" out of which nothing sensible can be understood, Theobald, in a studio that "savoured horribly of indigence," displays on his easel "a canvas that was a mere dead blank cracked and discolored by time." Unlike Frenhofer, who tosses Porbus and Poussin into the street, Theobald admits his "nullity" but adds, "Isn't it a promising foundation? The elements of it (the masterpiece) are all *here*!"—that "here" is a tapped forehead. Theobald acknowledges that he cannot translate what is in his head into his hand, that he is in effect an artist *manqué* whose conception has outstripped his ability; the poetic death by brain fever shortly after the narrator's visit reinforces the integrity of the trapped idea. Rather than overpainting, Theobald cannot begin, and yet the canvas is studied by both artist and visitor as if it were more than a work of art, as if it were a psychic event exhibiting a wholly modern sense of artistic failure. To our eyes the unprimed, stretched, gashed, and dusty canvas bears the significance of Duchampian commentary that at first sight would indicate tragedy, at second, farce, and during both a willed aesthetic shape. Yet that is not its potential in James's tale, though it approaches for the narrator the status of a sign bearing Theobald's name, in part because the issues of ideal philosophy are thematized in the absence of a single brushstroke that would inevitably destroy the perfect conception: Theobald lives and dies as his name suggests, nakedly godlike. In what sense does James read Balzac by this story, and to what degree does Theobald's *Madonna* further the dilemma of Frenhofer's *Catherine* for James himself, for his audience and for us as readers of both stories and both "errant" canvases? What remains in Balzac a problem in the psychology of the artist becomes for James a matter, in part at least, of philosophy; there is in the latter a respect for the doomed aspiration of art toward philosophical statement, a significance to the gesture of failure because it does not stray from the integrity of the universal idea, even at the cost of the artist's life. Theobald's *Madonna* is "of the future" in constituting an object not with regard to idealism alone but to the concept painting, a connection between the *technē* and significance that the issue of representation in Balzac cannot account for or fathom. The "human life" that Theobald's canvas signifies embraces the impossible gesture as its supreme statement, one that James will restate, revise and refine throughout his career, both in and out of the context of his artist tales. In this sense there is a qualitative semantic change between Balzac and James that enables us to read Theobald's canvas; the apparent two-way street in James means that there is a grammar within which Theobald's doom is neither a misunderstanding nor a madness and yet which cannot per se open the failure to an artistic tradition of the painterly. Truth and representation are categorically indistinct, though not in any sense that might lead one to misread, for example, Focillon in order to reconcile them: "A work of art's location in time does not define its principles nor the particularity of its form" (*Vie des formes,* 93). The signs of failure in Balzac and James do not change, nor does the desire toward artistic achievement; there is instead a shift of aesthetic grammar, an arc of modernity, whereby Theobald's empty canvas is present in a way Frenhofer's full one is not (and so must be displaced by the figure of the artist himself).

Grammatically speaking, representation is an originary trope signifying the necessity of translating pictorial into verbal phenomena without having to acknowledge either the movement or its complex consequences for the truth content of aesthetic analysis. The problem of representation serves as an arena for the institutional claims of truth content in the discursive treatment of pictorial objects, which has a happy and necessary by-product of finding in language a way for the most visually "inaccessible" works to be made readable. Whether representation is viewed dialectically or positivistically, within its categorical boundaries "windows on the world" and "mirrors of real signs" do not suffer the anxiety that must otherwise result from a confrontation with objects that might be characterized as not needing a spectator; language is always art's foremost audience. If "art is not required to understand itself," it is because we are able to analyze works either as they call attention to the debts they owe outside themselves visually or to the debt language owes them; the semantic "ineffability" of a painting is, in this sense, a failure of discourse. To this extent writing *about* art is writing art, and without the bearings of a self-consuming narrative in which the "otherness" of language would be apparent, there is, for example, essentially no ontological difference between Rilke, Fry and Shapiro on the subject of Cézanne.

While communities of interest enjoy the flux of cultural commerce, breakthroughs in the linguistic tradition as a self-comprehending totality face a retrenchable impersonality of principles. Within the ruse that viewers read a painting rather than language itself, the analysis of audience can take numerous forms, each of which negatively substitutes for or displaces the analysis of language that, with regard to truth content or the meaning of the object, ought to occur. Such a willful slippage enables the study of art to avoid skepticism toward its ontological, epistemological or methodological doxologies. Even ostensibly radical readings in new art history and visual theory take as their points of departure the trodden paths of authoritative categories; the disagreements, even viewed as heresies, lie in the realm of either targets for interpretation or the effect of modified methods on traditional concepts of realism, narrativity, expression, etc. Comparative studies between arts, in principle the most pragmatic site for the critique of institutional poetics, by tending toward a "ground" in one of literary, pictorial or musical representation aspire to little more than the quaintness

of analogy or discrediting traditions of genre-bound understanding; their implicit adherence to grammatical communities of
authority outside their avowed areas of "expertise" merely un-
derwrites the anxiety of meaning. Even so, estrangement from
an institutional training in art studies has provided some, Bryson and Danto among them, with methodologies (if not episte-
mologies) sufficiently "extraneous" to reliable forms that, as is
the case for Foucault, Marin, Derrida, Serres, Bernhard, and others, at least the "truth" of tacit manipulations can become apparent. And yet a "reinscription" of pictorial art within the greater
scope of theory's rhetorical analysis runs the risk of leaving
untouched the closeted skeleton of categorical imperatives:
while representation is newly problematized, its semantic com-
ponents undergo no invasive surgery. To this extent one must
yet attempt to read representation as a "language-game" whose
ur-history remains unwritten, whose grammar is either un-
charted or misplaced on the map. Even in the glossy debate
over Foucault's reading of Velázquez, in the elegant semiosis of
Bryson before still-life, and the quasi-Hegelian aspiration of art
toward philosophy reenfranchised by Danto, the primacy of
representation as the centered-ness of pictorial reading, reinter-
preted and re-created as it is, remains monolithically serene. In
a sense—to paraphrase the Velázquez debate—whether the mirror reflects royalty or its depiction on canvas, whether reflection only is reflected, whether subjectivity is elided, erased or
objectified, and whether the actual vanishing point pushes the
entire argument into the history of ideas rather than the history
of painting, that infamous redoubtable mirror cannot itself be a
painting among many others in the room because it is ulti-
mately the representational language that prevents the figures
in *Las Meninas* from looking at us. Just as Gadamer invents an
ontology for painting by distinguishing images in pictures from
those in mirrors, so do the traditions of reading art reflect a
unity of intentions in which the mirror, held to nature and even
to paintings, never ventures to place itself before itself.

By characterizing modernity as a theoretico-historical site for
the problematizing of representation, contemporary art readers
from Fried to Marin and beyond consider the modern in its episte-

mological aspect, as a method of knowing rather than as a condition of being; in this regard the relationship between the function of representation in our time and norms of tradition constitutes a modern poetics of pictorial analysis, reading painting as an encoding to be decoded and recoded in various versions of "dialectic" semiosis. This provides a locus for the study of art in which the discursive problem can be subsumed under the general consideration of the operation of different sign systems; as a theory of description, a semiotic poetics is able to enunciate "a system of operative rules that preside in making a work" (Eco). This differs from a grammar in the specific sense that a poetics assumes the subjectivity of composition to be the context of bringing the object nearer to our understanding; it "scientizes" the problem of the sign, its interpreter and the indeterminacies that history makes of both. There naturally remains a *frisson* between the reframed sign and the trace of its origins that fundamentally reinstates materiality within questions of realism, naturalism, etc., the virtue of which lies culture-bound even as it expands such categories as perceptualism and the psychology of seeing. To appropriate Marin's definition of historical painting, "time intelligibility in a spatial medium" exerts a force that draws to it not only the canvas itself but theories concerning how the canvas can be meaningful. The Marin quotation easily stands not only for the analysis of certain kinds of painting, but for the most insistent features in the foundation of art study itself.

Circularity, the embarrassment of modernism, holds sway in the revisioning of art analysis to the extent that while the autonomy of art is a dead authorial concept, its successor in the form of audience treads a similar path to arrive at a different destination—dissemination. Whether verbal or imagistic, reliance on etymology as a mode of knowlege (kin, in medieval thought, to rhetoric), whatever its enormous pedagogical virtues, returns us only as far as hermeneutics, mythography and tautology can take us; and without a concept of progress or utopia, dialectics becomes an archaism or formalism in the service of synthetic projections of order, or worse, an exercise in ornamented syllogism. It is the power of circularity that makes systematic thought appealing, even to the degree that, for example, Freud's misunderstanding of rudimentary embryology fails to quiet indefatigable combative debate; indeed it is the "fracture" that catalyzes rather than discredits. All discussions of representation suffer circularity to the degree that they must recall norms of perception, tradition, or identity for their credence. On the one hand, this is because of the mysterium the pictorial remains, and mysteries are problems, as Santayana said, that encroach on their own data. It would seem one can choose to believe myopia is clarity or, anathematically, view the horizon with vertigo. Danger in the latter is of course that one concludes in surrealism, a hysterical methodology in search of ontological closure.

To play chess, writes Wittgenstein, is to have all the rules in your head though you may not engage them. And though you may not use all the possible moves, you must know them—they must be hypothetical—in order to play the game. Out of the hypothetical, therefore, the actual emerges, meaning that the trace of a different use of a rule is contained as a necessary hypothesis of any one use. Only one state of affairs obtains at any one time, and while others do not, all are conceivable. By this example of the relationship between grammar and proposition, and by the strategy (it is not a metaphysic) that syntax is semantics ("the scaffold is the meaning"), Wittgenstein moves away from characterizing experience or event as reliant on representational correspondence for the creation of meaning. Grammar, or the "place, function and relationship of a proposition with respect to others in the same system," engages neither metaphysics nor subjectivity for the quality of its understanding. Grammar considers lateral connections exclusively, making no claims to recover lost objects (or thought) nor, equally pertinent, comprehending experience as cognitively coexistent with one's description of it. The "horizon" of grammar stands at the back of the reader's "as if," that position from which theories of imitation and correspondence become theories of representation. The intent of grammatical study is to scrutinize the relations between expressions of perception, cognition and truth content from the standpoint of each as distinct operations of language ordinarily totalized within a comprehensive concept of art reading; it is, to this extent, restricted to the consideration of implicit rules of language games that, absent of inquiry, artificially "naturalize" the nexus between art objects and their viewers.

The text to follow is neither deliberately fragmentary nor inherently radical; on the contrary, though it challenges the vocabulary of representation in part by arguing its inaptness in the study of abstract art (where extremes reveal the trace of a greater inadequacy), its unquiet and often internal disagreement bespeaks the contradictions between the need for new forms of discourse and the persistent need to address entrenched issues regarding perception, method and meaning. In essential ways its own perspective is polyglot, by which it is meant that there is no "ground" discourse in literature, philosophy, or art theory. It is avowedly an experiment always pointing toward; in this sense it is a drama, albeit muted and modest. Its actors—Wittgenstein, Pollock, Joyce, and modernity—exemplify not only extremes in modern grammar but for these purposes signify a crisis in the architectonics of discourse. A cautionary note, ineradicable from the text's foundation, may come from Augustine, who warns that using language to examine language creates the same confusion as rubbing one finger against the other to cure an itch: none but the sufferer knows which finger itches and which scratches.

Toward a Grammar of Abstraction

Grammar tells what kind of object anything is.
— Wittgenstein, *Philosophical Investigations*

1. How can one write about not understanding a painting? Is it possible for there to be a painting at all until it is understood?

2. When Benjamin writes that he can offer explanation but not understanding, he is saying that he can propose a grammar by which we could understand if we learned the rules. If the problem were the meaning of a painting, an explanation of the painting would enable us to experience it rather than merely see it. Experience is therefore learning a grammar; understanding is making use of one. A grammar, then, is an explanation. To *express* one's understanding requires moreover a different grammar, one that connects an object to an analysis. The difficulty in the case of Pollock may be that explanation and understanding conflate; it may be that we only understand the explanation and can only connect grammars. The sign may only be explained by a sign, so it can never be understood. Is this why, for example, when people view Pollock they see a landscape, a myth, a psychological statement by Jung, or a plate of pasta? They translate the experience of the painting into a language they already know, moving it from one verbal scene to another, or from a visual to a verbal, as though from a museum to a living room. This is not decoding Pollock, not a mode of understanding any more than is Rubin's seminal essay, which "accounts" for Pollock by a mosaic history of early modern-

ism. The various translations do not say that a Pollock says something, but that it says something *else,* or that it says something to them only when it is submitted to a familiar text. This practice neither explains nor understands, but rather places the painting within a different grammar, as though to admit there is either no grammar to Pollock (it is non-sense) or that a grammar is too difficult to learn. Nor is this practice an appropriation of the painting (in the poststructuralist sense) because it claims the understanding of meaning as its goal. It is the kind of understanding, however, we enjoy only during a dream in which we are able to speak an unknown foreign language fluently. On the other hand, as the critique of interpretation suggests, if I must decode the painting in order to understand it, do I understand the painting or the code? Similarly, if I admit that there is something unget-atable to the painting, an inexpressive something or other, why do I assume that this is the painting's most significant feature or greatest virtue, and the one that lovers of Pollock silently share against his detractors? Why should the unspeakable be a source of real joy, as though it presented to the viewer an article of faith? From the viewer's point of view, we might call it a matter of taste; from the painting's, mystery. Aura.

3. The line in a representational painting is different from the line in Pollock. To note and depart from Fried, in a representational painting the truth of the line depends upon our understanding of lines in the world, even if the line in the painting proves to be "inaccurate," as in the ceiling of Vermeer's *Allegory of Painting,* where, though they come toward the viewer, the lines do not thicken as they approach, nor do the spaces of ceiling between the lines widen as they do in reality. As soon as we perceive the discrepancy not only between the painting and our view of real ceilings, but between the painted ceiling's inaccuracy and the accuracy of other details in the Vermeer, we can read the significance of these "flawed" depictions. In the case of lines in Pollock, however, we can only speak of their "accuracy" as being the result of the painting's coherence or of their legibility according to a known grammar outside the painting; we can only recognize the lines according to what we take to be internal

rules or their translatability, in effect not that the lines make meaning but that they provoke a certain feeling in the viewer or implicate another vocabulary. An analogy to the difference might be that of the word book to the object book for the case of Vermeer, and for Pollock the English word *book* to the French word *livre*. This, however, is only an analogy, not an explanation. Does this mean, though, that the lines in Vermeer *refer* to lines in real ceilings, while those in Pollock *stand for* lines? Were Arnheim correct that the abstract line abstracts (withdraws from) the representational line, then would we say that the line in Pollock is an act of criticism, a substitution (a metaphorical line), a parody, or all three?

4. To say, as in modernist vocabulary, that Pollock *defamiliarizes* the line is to suggest that the line in his painting occurs in an unfamiliar visual space; that is, in a different pictorial grammar from the one in which it usually occurs. If the line in painting recalls to us the significance of drawing to painting, then the line tends toward the perfect line, whether straight, curved or circular. Just as straight lines evoke a correctness that rarely appears in nature, and therefore points to the human creation of objects, so the straight line in a painting is part of either a human object grammar or a grammar of humanized nature. The straight lines of the cubed trees at Schönbrunn Castle belong to a grammar of objects not found in nature but in architecture. As such they interrupt our identification of the trees; though this would be the case if the trees were "perfectly" triangular as well, it would be less so because we understand trees as more or less triangular. The perfectly triangular tree would evoke the geometrically truest tree, whereas the cubed tree evokes other kinds of objects. The cubed trees at Schönbrunn violate our definition of geometric treeness in a way, for example, that triangular tables do not simply because the latter are objects made for human use. We are puzzled not by the shape of tables, but rather by the number of their legs—a two-legged table may be baffling because we know it ought not to be stable enough for use. Just as the cubed trees at Schönbrunn occupy a different visual space from trees in nature because their shape is derived from a geometry based on human

use, so Pollock's line occupies a different visual space from pictorial line in general. It is intransitive drawing, which we consider abstractly expressive because it ostensibly moves private sensation into a public realm. Since our expectations of painting, like those of nature, are based on what we already know how to say, Pollock's line violates our grammar of the pictorial function of the line. So it is named writing, calligraphy or spaghetti, or we interpret Pollock's own relationship to it, understanding it as the act of production.

5. What of the assumption that the line in Pollock expresses feeling? Rather than consider the relation between sensation and feeling by asking *which* feeling does the line in Pollock express, one might wonder why, if the line expresses feeling, we don't simply consider feeling the meaning or function of the line. While the viewer experiences emotion before the painting, it is more accurate to say a feeling accompanies the line, or that the line, like a clothesline, is something on which to hang emotions. Once, however, we consider the line a *gesture* we indicate that its meaning is more refined than feeling or sensation, that it takes its place in relation not only to other uses of lines but to other kinds of gestures. As a gesture we may even consider the line a symptom, the way open flowers are a symptom of daylight, while the sun, for example, is a sign of it. In wondering at the status of the line, therefore, we cannot entirely avoid the baggage of emotions—but why do emotions seem to get in the way of meaning? If we can't really see the line as a sign, then what is its use? Is it a boundary? Is it a procedure? An explanation? Even if we assert that the line has a particular purpose and that it creates specific effects, that it is part of a mechanism, we cannot easily grasp the nature of the mechanism or its meaning. Is the line a notation the way a dot, if you will, is part of a musical composition? Then it must acknowledge criteria, there must be rules it obeys. Does this mean there is a model that it either follows or violates? Is the grammar of which it is a part a formula for something? That I can see a debt in Pollock's line to Klee or Kandinsky or Gorky helps to establish a grammar without explaining its purpose. That I fail to see in Frank Stella's line, for example, a debt to Pollock's line only aids me in understanding

Stella's grammar; it seems to have no bearing on my understanding of Pollock's.

6. If I feel the significance of Pollock's lines when I view one of the paintings, I am noting a difference between them and arbitrary marks on a canvas. I can feel only when influenced by the lines, and can only be influenced by experiencing a connection between the look of the lines and the guidance they exhibit. The lines appear justified, though in fact it might be that the justification, which enables me to speak of the lines, serves as the actual guide to their influence. In order to feel I have to conceptualize the ways in which influence occurs. I have to describe to myself a connection between seeing the lines as lines and being directed by them, at which point they are criteria. To understand a line, then, is to understand a painting: "The line intimates to me which way I am to go."

7. If the referent in Pollock is the line, then the borders of the line would indicate how the paintings cannot be fulfilled, first by noting that the lines do not circumscribe objects or essential forms. If the line appears as an intention without an object, what are the lines in its neighborhood other than the same? The lines cannot help but refer, point, but to what? The question implies a determination, not itself a referent or nature of the line, but rather a destination for it. If its destination were the center of the canvas, then we would understand it as originating at the edge and the matter of a frame would enter into the grammar as a measure of painterly orientation at least. In the case of Pollock, however, if the line's destination were the edge, we would still understand it as originating at the edge but wonder which one. We would have to presuppose not only the explanation in order to pose the question but, in the case of the line, presuppose the process of analysis as being essentially the same as the line (a dialogue of origin and destination). How do we treat the line as an object when it specifically circumscribes and informs nothing? The "there-is" seems particularly "with-drawn" from a Pollock line, as though it were the horizon of a dizzy drunk that could not be straightened in the morning—an observation edging dangerously close to a theme.

8. Pollock's marginal marks brought front but without center remain in history, though not in the history of the image. By viewing the paintings as excessively modified, do we suggest that Pollock paints allegories of a consciousness that presumed itself to be nature ("I am nature" he remarked), just as it presumed itself to be "in" the canvas when it did so? Of course the paintings have nothing to do with nature, anymore than walking around and on the canvas puts Pollock into it. The two claims remain indicators in the artist's rhetoric, an effort to draw a straight line between himself and the work. "I am nature" and "I am in the painting" suggest, logically at least, that nature is in the painting. Such an allegory is the result of Pollock's dissociation of thinking and feeling ("de Kooning thinks more, I feel more."); so he is saying he feels he is nature and he feels he is in the painting. Such feelings have nothing to do with a straight line for either artist or audience. They are efforts to suggest that his art and he are not incongruous. He is not simply known by his paintings, he is them, which makes of them false mirrors, because if he is nature he does not need to paint canvases. It is the fact that he cannot be nature that informs the paintings with the reality that they are not nature either. The failure of them as nature reveals their contingency, their deferred sense of truth. It may be that the paintings confuse script with statement, and therefore that anything in them can be anything else. What does it mean when Pollock asserts that his paintings are "making progress"? Is it that they are moving from disguised non-sense to clear non-sense? At once there are no accidents in the paintings, but no thinking either—this would imitate nature from Pollock's point of view.

9. Would Pollock have meant that such lines are in nature and he represented these, or that it was in his nature to paint such lines? Does he construct an ideal use for the ordinary line, as in scribbling, not so much better as refined, and in the process modified to extremes? What is an extreme line? In Pollock's case it might be the line that *in*scribes, that makes inscription, which determines the position not of alterity but of same with other: this line is different from that line in that they are related but not identical; each is unique but shares the same origin; each has a differ-

ent history but is constituted the same. The *mise en rapport,* however, is only realized when the lines exceed, without subordinating, each other. They are related only when they are not symmetrical. The re-mark that erases the mark embodies a crease (*le repli* that replies)—the environs of catastrophe theory in that it interrogates the potential for disaster in the line that ordinarily constitutes drawing. We cannot distinguish the outside or edge because that is all we see. How do such lines not arrive at a destination and still remain painting?

10. The "writeable" nature of Pollock's paintings derives not from their apparent commitment to subjectivity, but from their redundancy. They are rigidly labyrinthine in that the illusion of continuity always leads to an illusory dead-end. The repetition of connections and corrections is, in one regard, encyclopedic, and in another not far from computerization. The collapse of the line, informing all the possibilities of its fate, introduces into Pollock's grammar the logic of digression, the visual equivalent of the pun. What is more, the possibilities of the line can be said to construct Pollock's recapitulation of all paintings ever painted. Could one reconstitute from Pollock's line everything that came before it? It encompasses drawing without being it: the intensity of such a recapitulation provides the resistance of Pollock's painting to analysis, as though the viewer would have to speak of everything in order to speak of anything.

11. The line is always a line of argument, a horizon that detaches creation from its source; perhaps this disjunction expresses the significance of Pollock's separation of feeling from thought. Does he introduce time into abstract space by painting flow? Does *tempus fu(g)it?* What, in this context, causes the lines to happen (*arrive, passe*)? In their adventure across the canvas, Pollock's lines desire obstacles, perform evasive maneuvers against their destinies and predict their own catastrophes even as they seek their familial bonds. They appear to search out the other only to find themselves and their like; their excess is reminiscent of incest. Why else would the painter keep turning his work, or himself, now one way, now another, with no "right" side up, no

vertical or horizontal, no boundaries or taboos, until he cuts a length in order to pin it to a wall and thereby undo not only his own perspective but the direction of gravity? The lines that are cut on the canvas are also cut off the canvas, severed until the painting is called finished (all over). The painting digresses, unpenned, leaving a maplike work pointing to what is off the edge much in the manner by which cartography displaces landscape: castration as the punishment for incest.

12. In binary thinking we would say that the intertwining and overlapping lines present metaphoric catastrophe to metonymic meaning, if we were thinking binary. If a continuous line of black, say, were a statement, and that of gray another, the knotting of them would constitute a slip, three-dimensionally, of the sort we could associate with the emergence of the unconscious, which occupies a privileged position in Pollock readings. That the three-dimensionality would only be an illusion serves more to undo the unconscious as a successful metaphor than it does to bring it to the surface. Rather, it materializes it the way illusion is material effect—the lie that binds. Pollock's line seems destined for obstacles even while it has no clear destination; that is its illusionism. Were destiny the other end of the canvas (assuming we knew a source), a straight line would be not only more efficacious but truer. A scribble, however, is not a straight line in search of itself, nor an effort at precision gone awry. We can see, at one register, the ambivalence attached to the desire to know the other, an ambivalence that becomes the path itself, though a path to obstacles. A function of intertwining, of lines overlapping and lapping themselves, is to overcome, to continue, to establish a mnemonics of abstraction. Does such a drama of painting vocabulary constitute visual homonymy? If knot, then not? As in the Gordian not? Wittgenstein: "One observes in order to see what one would not see if one did not observe" (*Remarks on Colour*).

13. Jackson Pollock's line: Nile of the E/nil: the nonexistence the line as medium reserves for the line as object. The nonexistence of the line as object requires a grammar that reads redundancy yet avoids the standard line—psychobiography, mythography, te-

leology. Anaseme: the object as such never appears, but the story of its nonappearance can be recovered. Alloseme: linguistic *action* such as palindrome, anagram, acrostic, homography, pantography. Interlaced, anaseme and alloseme suggest how one must reread re-marks not in order to read meaning but, as in calligraphy, in order to read in the line the evidence that its motion began before the surface was touched and will end only after it has departed. Time is implicit in the calligraphic gesture. Dangerous note: Pollock's older brother, the one who introduced him to *Finnegans Wake,* was a calligrapher; his mother, moreover, sewed crazy-quilts.

14. Klee: "The dot takes time to become a line" (*Notebooks*).

15. When I analyze Pollock's line I seek a grammar with arbitrary rules (as in all grammars) but no accidents. Why the line? Are viewers of Pollock Nile-ists?

16. If to understand a painting means I know a way to interpret it, what is the effect on understanding of various interpretations, some of which I discard, others of which I am ignorant, still others of which I may not grasp if provided them? If understanding means I have a vocabulary for the painting, then there is a grammar whose origins, as well as application, provide the painting a text—historical, political, technical. The origins not only indicate the rules of the grammar but how and why those rules obtain rather than others. That is, the origins are not simply the background of an interpretive attitude but the only proof that the vocabulary is valid, or valid today. How many vocabularies to which Pollock has been subjected are the result of invalidated origins? The problem is one of trying to remember that the "when" of an interpretation is crucial to the usefulness of understanding; it is the *when* that offers a context to the *is* of the interpretation: for example, the painting is a mural, the painting is like a Kandinsky, the painting is about totemic myth, the painting is one of his best, the painting is a deconstruction of Picasso, the painting is from the late period. As each *is* inscribes the painting differently, recalling various interpretive origins, the ne-

gation of *is* offers greater possibilities of traceable grammars in which both *is* and *is not* may have valid substitutes, each of which in turn points to wholly different grammars. A choice signals a grammar and its origin, but as well the consequences attached to them for the possibilities an interpretation does not realize. Those other possibilities are formed when we speak of ambiguity, paradox and openness in a work. We account for rather than activate them; that is to say, we circumscribe a vocabulary with punctuation and let the punctuation stand for the frame of the analysis. Methods of interpretation are exercises in the placement of pointers. I can substitute words in an analysis and thereby change the meaning without altering either the syntax of sentences or the logic of the argument. The same structure can paint different pictures to different effects. This is only one way in which Pollock's paintings and the analysis of their grammar address one another.

17. What the effort to read Pollock has amounted to is the cancellation of the undecidability factor. The more the works undermine reading, the more a vocabulary impertinent to the visual field is brought to bear. That these vocabularies are essentially spatial in their relationships (mythography, dream, psychobiography, influence) indicates the extent to which readers universalize Pollock, exercise the urge toward totality that abstraction seems to articulate. The readings of Pollock dramatize the salient feature of modernist thought: the explanation of a totality by the creation of systemic substructures. In short, the more elusive Pollock's gestural marks, the more determinate are their readings, usually determinations attributed to the paintings themselves, as if the problem of a visual grammar did not exist.

18. The effect of determinate readings, like overdetermined paintings (allosemic, allover, "allalluvial"), is indeterminate. That the paintings suffer no referents but the language used about them points to the necessary ignorance they must exhibit in order to be full of knowledge eventually. Even in the fullest canvas, the language of analysis exceeds the painting. This is another way in which Pollock introduces time into abstraction,

not too distant either from *Le Livre* of Mallarmé, in which mathematical notation assumes the function of plot, but plot as perpetual prefigurations of readership. In both cases time signifies this much at least: correction. Are Pollock's homographs the scene of corrections? The appearance of improvisation requires a correctible structure that in fact only repetition can provide. The visual slips that occur as twinings and knots suggest a vertical depth, giving rise to spatial grammars, though the spirals, folds and cusps are the mathemes of the paintings' written associations, describing without explanation or echo a series of discontinuities. The pedagogical element in Pollock can be found in the density of his manipulation of a simple visual grammar. A concern for the unconscious, say, is a form of unknowing, an effort, as in Mallarmé's numerology, to "equalize" a viewer's requirements with his own; rather than aggravate the difficulty of reading, the motif or theme is there only to alleviate the manipulation and to democratize the density. Even if we cannot all paint, we share an unconscious, as good a point of departure for modernist understanding as any. Who is the painting for if not for us?

19. Lacan: "Writing is a trace in which is read an effect of language. It happens when you scribble something" (*Encore*). The "white writing" of Mark Tobey becomes in Pollock pantography (all-writing) not because the paintings deny the previous edge of the picture plane, as is Rosenberg's argument for the "all-over" characterization, but because irrespective of destination they exhibit lines as their exclusive content. The pun is clear: play the *pleine* plane plain.

20. The idea that his work is a product of inspired frenzy has influenced the study of his paintings in a way that, for example, preempts the consideration of precision, of draftsmanship. Even if he arrives at the "right" solution to a problem in a painting, Pollock appears as an artist who cannot know how he got there. The argument that Pollock's painting transparently expresses sensation and inner experience relieves his readers of the need to calculate a grammar: accents, volumes, registers, nouns, verbs, flatten out in the face of his "private use" of primitive material.

Rather than accept the assumption that Pollock is a lyrical painter, one might treat the work as epic, composed of public material and executed with the calculation of an architect, despite the artist's own words and the paintings' titles (which were given by friends of Pollock). The paintings are a black hole of modernism and the big bang of the postmodern—merely one of the connections to *Finnegans Wake.*

21. Proposition: We can discuss Pollock's allosemic paintings without referring to any one of them in particular. It is as though they are something other than paintings but, unlike conceptual art, are more "painted" than most other paintings. Do we think they stand for something more than other paintings? And do we think they stand for something more than most other paintings because they do not refer to objects in the world? If so, is it because their visual effect is at once unambiguous and material—lacking nuance? It would seem that Pollock's work is unambiguously the "lateral displacement" we associate today with grammatology. However, the search for a grammar intends no reference to that activity; the association is verbally sensual only, not theoretical. But then that is a feature of grammatology.

22. What makes Pollock's method of painting modernist is not the novelty, though that is how it is often approached, but the pastiche, the bricolage of it. Not only does he mix common detritus with house paint, but he merges techniques as well (Duchamp with Navajo, for example). His material and application are equally quotations. In this sense he refines the idea of tradition: by adding to the arrangement of quotations the critique of techniques, Pollock elaborates the material definition of "painterly" tradition. While not imitating, for example, Picasso's use of primitive imagery, he is able, by Picasso's example, to make use of the concept, indeed to elaborate it by adopting ancient drawing methods. If I say that the puzzle for viewers of Pollock lay in the fact that though his work seems indisputably "correct" we don't know how to apply the term, I mean that we don't know in what sense its aptness means anything. The literal function attached to "the painting makes a statement" is con-

fused in Pollock because we cannot seem to make one ourselves. Is it apt to say that his paintings do not want to begin a dialogue? Are they "*détours de force*"? Or is this just a way of saying that we focus on the fulfilment or frustration of our expectations, that any artwork is defined by those alternatives? The painting may be apt but, to me at least, not very good; if I know it is apt I also know that someone somewhere will think it is good and they will be right. This too is a part of my expectation, though it does not diminish my surprise that a painter could persist for fifty years, say, without my liking a single work. These two ideas are not incompatible, but of different types.

23. To an extent the problem of a Pollock grammar has been forestalled by a doubt as to whether his work is painting. Aside from the fact that it hangs on a wall, a Pollock work seems to provide an unmediated visual experience, a pure sensorium, as though unlike other great artwork it does not direct us to an appropriate way of viewing out of all the possibilities. In this a Pollock behaves like an ordinary object in the world, indifferent to our identification of it, the way a jar, for example, can be read as an amphora, a pitcher, a visual pun, an image out of Wallace Stevens, without intruding on the recognition of the jar. No one would question the validity of seeing the jar in various ways while knowing at the same time that an interpretation of it is not necessary. The two ways of seeing—unmediated and mediated— do not interfere with each other. Pollock's lines may or may not induce us to imagine figures or objects without suffering in our judgment because of it. We cannot say the same of Rothko, for example, or of any color-field painting—we know we must do something with it, that it is an invitation or occasion; its visual elements are too "simple" to elude contemplation. One may like or understand color-field but not because it is puzzling. And though its features are different, the same is true for de Kooning, in part because we instantly recognize brushstrokes the size of a house-painter's brush, whether or not we find in the paintings abstract readings of Dutch masterworks, for instance. Rothko and de Kooning facilitate reading, encourage "relating" to their works. We sense in them an "aim" that Pollock's density, for

example, questions. Fascination with Pollock's method only fuels the doubt; one always seems to be waiting to interpret. Perhaps that is why Pollocks are more often compared than analyzed, or when analyzed become allegories of mind or of the material conditions of painting, views that concerning almost anyone else would tend to be mutually exclusive rather than harmonious.

24. Focusing on Pollock's method displaces the perceptual problems his paintings create for the viewer. Knowing his method seems to permit an access to the paintings that the paintings appear to deny. Pollock's physicality is never far from a consideration of the work; it is as though if we know that he walked around and on the canvas we will be less frustrated as viewers trying to find a position for ourselves in front of it. Do we suspect he is trying to depict something but cannot? What fate awaits intention when a painting composed on a floor is exhibited on a wall? When a painting done from God's vantage is seen according to a mortal horizon of vision? Does this perhaps account for the "hostility" Pollock's work often generates even now? Are we not welcome before the paintings, or do we stand like sightseers made remote by sensory overload? Note, in this regard, that Pollock felt the force of a painting's center so completely that he erased the frame—a piece of furniture—that draws the viewer to it.

25. Reframed: "The symbol of crossed lines cannot be, to be sure, a merely negative symbol of crossing out. Rather it points into the four areas of the quadrangle and of their gathering at the point of intersection" (Derrida *Dissemination,* 354). The crossed lines, the chiasmus, the butterfly of catastrophe theory, also symbolize the angle of vision of a viewer to a painting. In Benjamin's terms, the crossed lines of the angle of vision indicate as well the history of the object; as he puts it, aura is the result of an object's sense of being looked at. The painting looks looked at.

26. How do I analyze my own understanding? Can I apply the same rules to it that generated it in the first place? Is there, as a result of understanding, a distance I have from it that becomes a

part of the grammar that would analyze it? How would I describe the distance except as the experience of using my understanding? If I could observe my understanding in order to analyze it the way I observe a painting, would the act of observation create what is being observed? Is this the case with a painting? Wouldn't I always be refining my understanding by analyzing it and therefore changing the object before me? This can occur with a painting because the grammar of it emerges only with my understanding. How would the grammar of the painting be affected by my analysis of my understanding? Could I prove both my understanding and the grammar of the painting inadequate at the same time? Is that why we seek another grammar by which to measure the painting without another by which to measure our understanding? Are lines on Pollock's lines a Nile themselves on the E/nil? On the nonexistence the line as medium reserves for the line as object? Do lines on Pollock's lines dramatize this nonexistence as well? In catastrophe theory (turning completely, misturning, turning down) a straight line signifies *being,* and yet there are no objects within the theory, only a method (*hodos,* road) of knowing, only an action of a specific grammar. In René Thom's grammar, then, Pollock's paintings do not exhibit *being,* yet they exist; would this make them semantic only because they are syntactic or would they otherwise be "philosophical" objects without metaphysical possibilities?

27. What are the criteria for understanding from the point of view of a grammar that would make understanding possible? One thing is certain: we think in the present, and everyone who thought before us expected us to do so.

28. On understanding and discourse: In an unwritten dialogue between Benjamin and Lacan, it is the case that the gaze of the subject does not require discourse so much as simple description, including description of the deceptive practices of the psyche; it is the gaze of the object (locus of the "aura" or sense of objects themselves bearing a gaze, gazing back) that demands or makes discourse possible; for example, the loss of the aura in the case of Benjamin. Is it in this sense, then, that the painting is

not a painting until there is discourse? And does that discourse describe or dramatize the gaze? Is it a ruse, a diversion (rather than digression) from the alienating effect of the gaze? Are we safer interrogating the reflected gaze in the Velázquez mirror, for example, than the gaze of the dwarf, the princess, the painter, even the dog because *in truth* the gazes of the king and queen are only inadvertently directed toward us and are in fact directed specifically toward king and queen themselves in much the way the Medusa's gaze is specifically directed toward itself in the ruse of the polished shield of Perseus? Would this, then, be Velázquez's Perseid? Returning to the Benjamin-Lacan dialogue, the former constitutes a historical gaze (cf. the image of the Angelus Novus), the latter psychological, both subject to analysis within the philosophy of reflection in part because of their foregrounding of discourse as symptomatic. The philosophy of reflection establishes not only the rules of, say, reading Hegel's ruse of consciousness, but it enacts it; in this way, reflection never is only descriptive but performative (tradition, as a concept, should be viewed in this way). A valuable analysis of surrealism as a procedure in modernist thinking would subject Benjamin's notion of aura to the Lacanian gaze; since both thinkers were "formed" by surrealism, such a treatment would enable us to understand the desire to characterize what objects "saw" in their heyday. But this proceeds from the belief that the concept of aura itself is a "misreading" of the Lacanian gaze before Lacan invents it. This is the stuff essays are built on (but not this one).

29. What would constitute a false grammar for the study of Pollock's painting? Understanding antecedents to his work as causes or origins would be to privilege continuity in the history of painting as an attribute of the work. Confusing understanding of the work with the construction of a totality for the history of abstraction might take us as far back as Cimabue's red line of blood in his crucifixion painting; that is, finding discontinuities in iconic paintings from which we abstract an abstract source of abstraction. Why stop there? Why not appropriate, for example, the depictions of Mary Magdalene's hair in paintings of the early Middle Ages

(calling them scribbles)? In short, how is the grammar delimited so that not simply any instance of abstraction would be a feature of a tradition? Can we speak of historical limits as well as those imbedded in a given genre? Which associations between the historical and theoretical are valid and which are not? What criteria are to be established and what criteria or experience or desire establish those? If I say that in Pollock lies the trace of Cimabue, am I saying something about Pollock's paintings or about my criteria for the development of abstraction? What additional rules, if any, play a role in the designation of an abstract moment? Would we seek slippage out of another genre, a matter of nuance? But nuance is not a part of grammar, it is a judgment that accompanies understanding. We would have to understand the line of blood in Cimabue (serpent? pure painterly occasion?) as a sign embodying the grammar of abstraction. Can I make such a case, given that the "painting" of a red line (again, the scribble) is a detail on Christ's palm, affording the viewer a perspective that not only abstracts the crucifixion but "prefigures" a zoom lens in photography? That is, would a detail in an iconic painting qualify as an example of abstraction? If not, why not, since of late we have come to "verify" the truth of abstraction as a representation of nature with the use of microphotography? What prevents us from saying that Pollock is a painter of quantum mechanics? In this I am applying a language rather than interpreting the signs so as to make an application possible, credible. On the other hand, by noting the vocabulary of physics or optics I am describing the conditions for comparing Pollock's paintings to grammars of reality.

30. Or, what is the difference in the trace of abstraction between Cimabue's serpent of blood and Vermeer's inaccurate ceiling in the *Allegory of Painting*? Is the Cimabue an abstraction because the serpent is *obviously* only a red scribble that need not conclude anywhere within the borders of the painting? Are we certain in the same way that the "failure" of perspective in the Vermeer abstracts from reality? Both moments depend upon perspective, though the Cimabue is a more startling instance in that we must imagine ourselves at an extraordinarily intimate proximity to Christ's palm even as the palm would

remain inhumanly large—it would not be merely a detail but, as for pedagogical study, an enlargement. The Vermeer would have to provide a super-subtle instance, which the Cimabue does not, and which the isolation of other details in Vermeer, for example, also would not. That is to say, the moment of abstraction in the Vermeer ceiling depends upon our seeing it as a ceiling that is incorrectly drawn, whereas the serpent in Cimabue and drapery, let us say, in Vermeer require no characterizations at all. The same cannot be said for the instances of blood in Mazzoto's crucifixion because they run along the feet of Christ the way blood in reality runs. Mazzoto obviously depicts the running of blood which it does not require the feet to be Christ's in order for us to recognize. In contrast, Cimabue's iconic blood can only belong to Christ. Perhaps Christ, in that case, is the source of abstraction.

31. If we make "sense" of the painting in order to speak of it, then we must ask what sort of sense language requires? Is there more than one sense that can be fashioned once we question the limitations that sense as coordination, as lateral thinking, places on the language we assume to be adequate? This reflects the doubt within language raised by its different uses: ordinary, aesthetic, logical. The instrumentation of language determines the "consciousness" of the painting; another instrumentation can render the first projection of sense false, not just alternate. Or if not false, then non-sense. Why, in analysis, should non-sense as a description be less meaningful than sense since sense, in the more conservative view, will always adhere to judgment that has nothing to do with the world of the painting. Even if we would not desire to remove subjectivity from the world of the painting, how would we do it since aesthetics is, philosophically speaking, still mystical?

32. In the case of Pollock's paintings, we cannot equate the sort of "reflexive" knowledge that constitutes their operations (or allusions) with the meaning of them anymore than we can establish a psychology for the paintings by referring them to psychoanalytic readings. Though we can analyze a geometrics of structure and a

grammar of line, we cannot translate these into the meaning of the painting: when one reconstructs the painting by relating its similar features as coordinates rather than recognizing that this is the site of the crisis (the horizon from which we perceive the problem), one is peremptorily unifying the "consciousness" of the painting by reading it as an abstraction of things in the world (tables, thoughts, other paintings), projecting it as a representation of representation rather than facing the crisis of representation it factually comprises. How do the constituent elements signify anything? If they are a sign, a priori, what are they a sign of? Two ways of posing the question: How can we read the complex before we read the simple? Why do we consider unity as meaningful rather than the extreme limits against which unity would appear, as a projection, to stand? Or, more important, why isn't unity perceived as the extreme limit of understanding, indeed the transcendent experience of the work rather than the *donnée* that allows the work to be meaningful?

33. In this regard, let us consider the subject Pollock. The painter becomes the subject/voice/author of his paintings when the paintings arrive at a place in a traceable tradition. The credulousness toward subjectivity in a *genus* marks the establishment of a living artist as a definition of the work he produces. Where there is no representation of things in the world, there is instead the presentation of a subject that does not represent things in the world; by that route, Pollock himself becomes a thing in the world according to his paintings. What is more, a thing like all other things that are capable of representing things in the world, whether they choose to do so or not. The underlying myth here is that the living artist's consciousness is a unity and thus the most successful paintings reveal or express the occasions when "things come together." But of what does this unity consist if not, inferentially, the vocabulary of a readership that already values unification, totality, as the intention and effect of the work of art? This urge is not escaped even in "inherently" fragmented works because the fragments remain measured as critiques of totality: fragments of the vessel are still perceived as fragments of a broken whole.

34. When do we understand a painting—while we are seeing it, after, when we are seeing other paintings as well? How can we understand a painting *before* we have seen it? The letter from a friend in Africa describing a rhinoceros served Dürer as the basis for his famous drawing; its writer presumed Dürer would understand the sense of the animal because he understood language. Because the sentences made descriptive sense of an absurd image—in effect, there need not have been a real rhinoceros at all—Dürer could understand the rhino before he saw it. In fact, though he could not have been certain, Dürer did not see a rhinoceros until he had drawn one. The language of criticism in painting serves a similar function, enabling us to make sense of what the eye may experience whether or not the eye translates images, color, composition per se into those known as a painting.

35. Two viewers of a painting can enjoy or experience it equally, yet one knows more about technique, tradition and the painter's other (greater or lesser) works. The "educated" viewer has more hypothetical paintings at his command, can multiply the poetics of the painting's possibilities; another way of speaking is that educated viewers have more knowledge of what the painting is "like" and "unlike." They therefore *understand* the painting better because they know more examples of more rules that govern not only painting in general but how others understand them even if the particular painting does not exhibit those rules. However, would understanding the painting privilege brushwork, say, more than the tradition of myth the painting portrays? Which would characterize the painting more, its painterly features or its pictorial ones? That is to say, there are more sign systems to master than the painting exhibits in order to understand the painting. Which ones? Would they, for example, always be collateral or, as in the case of this study, could they be systems or paradigms that read from different horizons? If I am applying a model that possesses no analogy to painting, is that like reading set theory (or catastrophe theory) as if it were a narrative? And would such an application suggest greater education about either the individual painting or painting in general? If we say that it would prove not pertinent, would not help us understand the

painting *qua* painting, would we reply that psychoanalysis, however, does help us because it actually does so or because we already understand psychoanalysis as collateral with painting? And in that specific case, though theories of perception and of optics would provide an even more disturbing problem vis-à-vis our ordinary looking at a painting, the source of lateral thinking would be nothing more than the common subjectivity of painter and reader, which, in order to seem pertinent, would have to avoid entirely the philosophical (or even psychological) issue of subjectivity. This is why we return time and again to the analysis of coding, decoding and recoding as processes, and why we must do so from the viewpoint of questioning those codes rather than assuming their efficacy as sign systems reflecting something other than themselves. Is the analysis of effect, of readership, really less solipsistic and mysterious than the analysis of cause and intentionality?

36. A "wheel of cheese" describes the form the cheese takes, but since a wheel as a mechanism must be hard in order to function, a wheel of cheese reduces the function to that of a picture. The Freudian dream process, an exemplary code, is similar in that the dream itself is a picture process whose mechanisms only become apparent when made to function by an outside force (the analyst); what the force must do is accomplish an explanation acceptable to the dreamer ("So this is what I meant!") in order for the mechanism to be validated. If the explanation is not sufficient for the dreamer, it cannot be true of the dream. The analyst's only authority for the aptness of the explanation is statistical; the neatness (totality) of the explanation has little to do with the dream itself but with the relationship of the explanation to its success in convincing the dreamer of what has not been previously apparent. Why, though, should the dream mean something other than itself in order to be meaningful to the dreamer? The sign system of Freudian dream analysis is of such an intentionalism that the slightest dilation collapses the whole of the explanation. As with all totalizing mechanisms, in Freudian dream theory, to learn anything, we must learn everything; if we learn less than everything, we have learned nothing except the

inadequacy of the sign system in relation to the picture. Yet we do not read codes in this way, and are not discouraged by their inadequacies; indeed, their gaps may serve as means of applying such codes onto other ambiguous texts (literature, for example). Discursive knowledge, as this process could be called, is what we derive from the "wheel of cheese," but not from the wheel. What sort of knowledge do we derive by avoiding totalization mechanisms, which are after all psychically as well as cosmologically satisfying? Or, what sorts of order are possible without thinking of unity?

37. If the effect of the explanation of the picture leads the reader to reject the picture, there is no further problem (except for the picture itself, whose sense has been lost). However, if the explanation is misunderstood (for example, Lacan means *penis* when he says *phallus*), then the effect will be different and the painting will have a different sense, though not necessarily a wrong one, than the explanation intended to convey. But if the effect of the explanation is satisfactory, then the reader, like the dreamer, will seek a cause to unify the meaning of the picture. The cause, though, will be coded within a different sign system disguised as a feature of the same or as contiguous (we can understand effects without thinking of causes, but thinking of causes requires effects). The lateral meanings that made the explanation affective necessarily continue in order to create an apt unity—explanations must bump in order to be read as cause and effect. The totality functions therefore by transforming the "this means something else" into "this only means this something else" without the reader knowing the transformation has occurred—that one sign system has been displaced by another in order for both to appear either the same or continuous. This process can be understood as a *deterioration* of the picture on behalf of the integration of effects, explanations and causes. The deterioration then would be the development of the picture's meaning. An alternative reading—fragmentation, for example— is not viewed as an explanation but only as another picture, a visualization of a visual phenomenon, a parasite confined to the philosophy of reflection and its reflexive generation.

38. Even as we revalue fragmentation—now viewing most of the arts as consciously opposed to unification—we do so from the standpoint of either a lost or illusory but no less desirable totality, as if either in history, myth or the purest theory there is or once was a tidy reconciliation of contradictions. Why would this be desirable if not to make mystery into explanation?

39. The reason that "thinking about painting" is like talking to oneself is that what we have come to consider painting is what we have learned, as a language, to say in the presence of a painted object. We guess at the value of a painting until we learn that it is valuable, after which we are looking for either similar paintings or familiar means of addressing dissimilar paintings in order to consider them of value. Just as we artificially erase the outline of an object in order to enjoy the color of it, so do we bracket the characteristics that separate paintings in order to value them. This primitive way of reading holds sway because many readers possess ostensive definitions of painting without realizing they are proceeding from definitions of value. Value, of course, originates in the experience of recurrence, seeing enough of the same sort of painting so that it becomes characteristic. Ascribing value is the product of pointing; therefore one says "that is painting" without necessarily meaning "that is *a* painting."

40. The problem of recognizing a painting grows complicated when we compare "this is a painting" to "this is a bad painting." A slab of wood with one leg in a corner is not a bad table, it is simply not one. A typewriter without keys cannot be a typewriter to someone who has no experience with typewriters in general, but is a broken typewriter to someone who knows how a typewriter works. The word *this,* the sign of an arrow, does not name something so much as indicate some sort of meaning to its predicate, regardless of what we do or do not know about the object without the *this.* Phrased in that way, isn't it possible to say that there are no bad paintings, but there are objects with paint on them? That is to say, the bad painting does not exist in its own right because it always demands not only an example to point to but its opposite—in either instance the *this* of the bad

painting needs a measure other than itself. "Now this is a painting!" at one register means the object exists as a painting in its own right; it can be named, though the *this* in such a case only indicates the name painting exists, or a quality called painting. Would one say it exhibits *Dasein?* Language is able to represent it.

41. Wittgenstein: "What *can* be shown *cannot* be said" (*Tractatus,* 4.1212). This is the heart of the problem of writing about art, which if considered rigorously would leave us in the position of either writing about the problem or revealing that what has been written about art are mere remarks, even when the latter appear within a system that accounts for the "transcendent" nature of all aesthetics. The question is not only of what sort of propositions do paintings consist, but what sort of propositions are made about paintings? We know that language cannot mirror painting, but it is harder to recognize that language cannot mirror its own forms of representing paintings or mirror its own forms of representing the problem of representing painting. It would seem to leave us in that place where there is either silence or where we venture on high while pulling the ladder up behind us—the place of either mysticism or the senseless (the critique of language). We have, perhaps, a site without an object, a locus suggested by the Homeric verb *therkesthatai* ("to look, at nothing, with longing"), and which ended with the epic. To pose the question another way: if we cannot speak logically about painting, how can we speak of it? If we have not been speaking logically, how have we? To what end? That is, knowledge with regard to painting is always possible; if not, none of us could ever speak of painting. But the meaning of painting, a *mysterium,* can never be the subject of writing about painting when knowledge is a ratio for understanding.

42. This notion requires grafting onto the statement by Roman Jakobson that "parallelism is the characteristic of all artifice." He means by this, without acknowledging it, that we interpret signs by recovering explicit or implied similarities between one sign and another, which is different from Stravinsky's remark (noted

by Jakobson) that similarity is the guiding principle in the composition of music. Jakobson conflates reading and writing along the
lines of parallel longings for parallelisms. The matter of having to
learn when a painting is present in order to name future paintings demands a look at the flaw in Jakobson's thinking. He proceeds from the need for a fundamental or originary sign in order
to index which system of similarities constitutes a work of art
and which might, for example, comprise a philosophical statement, therefore not a work of art. Uncovering allusive or familial
references among a group of words does not alone make them a
work of art; nor does Jakobson account for his assertion that it is
parallelism which offers the guide to totalizing words into a work
of art. At best one can say that parallelism is a technique for
thinking about works of art, indeed one of the indices we might
be said to learn in order to recognize art. While Jakobson intends
his statement as a description, he is in fact invoking judgment;
rather than describing how art works, or fails to, or how it cannot
be described, he assumes a source for artistic understanding no
less dubious than universalism and only slightly less absolute.
Parallelism within a single text or as a measure of intertextualism
is, to borrow a phrase of Adorno, the Wurlitzer organ of binarism
in aesthetic thinking.

43. "The seriality of totality introduces the consideration of
time, which is excluded from the genre of logic. There are,
though, logics of time that at least allow for this aspect of the
litigation to be made evident" (Lyotard, *The Differend,* 7). A part
of the problem of constructing a Pollock grammar lies in the
dispute between the line as a sign of temporal logic and the line
as a sign of the irrational. Writing about Pollock presumes one or
the other position as already *litigated,* when in fact what is
needed is a trial of the evidence and only after the rules of
evidence have been established. The modest goal of grammar
then is to establish the rules of evidence; a philosophical inquiry
is nothing more than a plenary session.

44. The mythic character of the mythic reading, the technicity
of the technical reading, the aestheticism of the reading-into-

traditions—all these predilections (motives, motifs) of analyses (interpretive as well as descriptive) presume the virtues of the conceptual frames without divulging the argument concerning their origins, if those who use them know them. It is not the absence of a conceptual etymology (Heidegger's corrective purpose in the development of hermeneutics) that obscures the actual "readings" such analyses perform. What has been a problem for philosophy, say, is suddenly not for psychoanalysis; for historiography suddenly not for the explication of a single work as paradigm; and so on. The wholesale removal of a framework from its work-frame (I do not mean the separation of form from content) succinctly eliminates the troublesomeness of doubt, which constitutes the failure of interpretive "reasoning." Readings then stand as valorized simply because myth functions, techniques exhibit themselves, traditions are received. Out of these nothing can come but the reiteration of the issues the concepts as points of legitimate departure originally raise. A temporal illogic then can be located in the consequence that canonical readings have the double security of at once being themselves models of understanding while pronouncing a *noli me tangere* upon their sources and origins.

45. If I am subjecting Pollock to an analysis *along the lines* of the relationship between early and late Wittgenstein (drawing the line not only there with philosophy, but drawing the line of Wittgenstein's philosophy), am I viewing them as somehow connected or am I *artificially* disputing one with the other, and if the latter, what is the difference? Would discontinuity result in less understanding than continuity? That is, a certain collision must be involved in the choice, even though or because, for example, Wittgenstein left aesthetics to the realm of the mystical, of which he could not write because he could not write logically. Wittgenstein often used randomly curved lines ("squiggles") as examples of meaninglessness because even if referred to other similar examples the squiggle would not make more sense (we would not know difference in the way we do between two drawings of faces). This does not imply that the squiggle is mystical, nor that it can be verified true or false, but rather that it cannot

make meaning. In short, I am as well submitting Wittgenstein to Pollock in order to consider the implications of Wittgenstein's assertion—"What *can* be shown *cannot* be stated." The fact that much of Wittgenstein's writing relies upon showing (e.g., the picture theory, the language games) necessitates understanding the position of the visual in his thought the way the space of the king on a chessboard, rather than the piece we call the king, is the meaning of the king in the *Tractatus.* By asking what method of spatialization serves to relate Pollock and Wittgenstein, I am first of all recalling that account of meaning. Is grammar impossible outside of it, since Wittgenstein's assertion is arguable? There can be no meaning without a grammar, and where there is a grammar there must be meaning—this is the consequence of Wittgenstein's position, the import of which to art theory has not been recovered, unless one wants to conclude that in the realm of aesthetics either Kant or Moore's critique of Kant brought his thinking to a standstill. His position might refer to the solipsism he termed microcosm, the self-limited world bordered by the inexpressible, by the shown, as though the picture of the world were external to thought but the writing of it not.

46. The scene of the line in painting originates in a primitive idea of the line's function, that is, as a line of communication, something joining one *thing* to another either in simple geometry or in terms of cause and effect as it travels in one direction only, as it *progresses.* The "equipmental" nature of the line (in Heidegger's sense) becomes the image of reason; logical thought has its empirical origins before it impinges on any rhetorical forms it might also embody. As to the line as *via negativa,* which might characterize at one register the line in abstraction (thought or painting, or even the literal definition of *cliché* as photographic negative), we learn to understand the line that is not reasonable by seeking others like it with which we are familiar. How, in short, do we conceive the meaning of a line that cannot be attached to anything we know, even to itself to form a circle? That is not a line, it is a scribble (Lacan), squiggle (Wittgenstein), "sexophonolinguistic schizophrenesis" (Joyce)—because it does not behave as a conjunction or as a distinction except with regard to what it is not. The *via*

negativa of the scribble retains the trace of the rational function of the line, of the line as rational sign, embodying at most the skepticism of the pyrrhic philosopher and thereby pointing toward the border between the known and the unknown, for example, conscious and unconscious, linear and spatial, presence and lack. The scribble then refers to the line the way a pillar refers to a slab without signifying the same thing. The scribble is at first the tool in a modified state to the extent that it only non-sensically relates to things other than itself. At another register its name indicates now its otherness to the line, its inutility as a line. If I say the scribble is merely another kind of line, I am accounting for (limiting it to) its "digressive" character. We can draw a straight line thinly or thickly without its function being altered, just as singing a note loudly or softly will not affect the note. The scribble, on the other hand, is similar to asserting something but beginning with "I believe."

47. In what way can I say the scribble parodies (or even acts upon) the line at the same time (in the same space) that it is ostensively (cf. Russell on ostensive definition and Wittgenstein's critique) not one? Were it a matter to be explained by a theory of solipsism, as though the scribble indicated a limited world, then one would have to explore why children first scribble without being taught, then, being educated to draw a straight line, privilege the ability to draw one without a hard edge for aid. That is, knowing how to scribble is not knowing the world in its instrumentality; scribbling is not meaningful, is a deterrent to knowledge of the world. This is not even similar to explaining the value of metaphor to a child. The scribble bounds the world between something meaning something to everybody and still meaning something else to me.

48. Boundaries as a feature of a Pollock grammar means that boundaries have a special purpose there that they will not have elsewhere, though they must have purpose elsewhere in order to be a feature of a Pollock grammar; it would otherwise be inconceivable. That is, while we can say that all paintings are in some ways bounded, to draw boundaries in the case of Pollock is to circumscribe not only his paintings in a specific way but to under-

stand boundaries in the limited sense his paintings draw them, no matter how wide that limited sense might be in his or any other painter's work. So boundaries in a Pollock grammar would include the absence of a frame, the allosemic picture plane, the application of catastrophe theory, but also the analysis of the line proper; while constituting examples of meta-boundaries (theoretical *mises-en-abŷme*) in themselves, lines alone belong beside the analysis of the line as part of the vocabulary of boundaries, as well as differing line functions. The features of boundaries in Pollock may, therefore, have little in common with boundaries in other painters' work, even if other painters observe a similar irony in the idea of boundaries; but among the features of boundaries in Pollock's work there must be the lacing of lines with themselves and these with boundaries as an idea. This is categorically different from considering how Pollock approached boundaries in relationship to Vermeer, Velázquez, Rothko, etc. It is not a question of how he approached an issue common to other painters, or in fact that he even did, but rather the limited sense of boundaries *named* in Pollock. Named boundaries is not the same as the meaning of boundaries, which would eventually require reference to boundaries in some other painter, even if an anonymous cave-dweller who, unlike Pollock, had lived in Europe. To name the boundaries is not to treat their meanings but to say simply that meanings might exist if we (and perhaps other painters) know boundaries in the world or in other paintings. But we could not proceed by starting with a definition of boundaries borrowed from elsewhere; there cannot, in the grammar, be boundaries in general.

49. By leaping boundaries in the discussion of art in order to create (the boundaries of) a grammar that discussions of art seem to have ignored, I am not indicating reasons for boundaries at all. They may be, depending on the reader of the text or of the painting, proprietary rules or rules of a game or temporal physics; they may make sense in one context but not in another. There is a difference in saying, "This discourse is the sign for reading a painting by Pollock" and "If I say such and such, then a Pollock painting must be present." I do not have to know the purpose of boundaries in order to draw them, not even whether

they will have the effect of preventing certain ideas, certain paintings and certain ideas of paintings from getting out of or into the discussion or the grammar. There is no outer and inner to the grammar anymore than there is to the discussion of it. Causal relations in an inquiry about painting and language do not have to be invented anymore than they do or do not have to be doubted. Boundaries identify conventions of reading whether the argument is carried on inside or outside them. Their limits, in their limited sense of Pollock's boundaries, do not pertain to truth or to meaning but to the existence and nonexistence of signposts within discrete communities of thought. When such communities ("constellations," in Benjamin's terms) overlap in the guise of parallelism, continuity, contiguity, or natural affinity, then it is important to point out that communities are prone to invasion by other communities (the idea of the mosaic, again in Benjamin's sense). A new discourse may be created in this manner, but it remains an arbitrary linguistic activity rather than the explication of linguistic possibilities within discrete communities. A problem for painting, or for a philosophy of painting (if any such philosophy exists), is not solved by thinking things through a series of Venn diagrams—that is to create new problems instead, itself a valid task but not that of a grammar. Grammar, on the other hand, must offer choices that can lead to statements; we learn the choices by posing questions; questions are bounded by replies (*les replis*).

50. The inquiry into a Pollock grammar does not include what such a grammar can enunciate but only by what means enunciation takes place. Grammar itself is not an interpretive tool at all, nor a historiographer's, etc.; the grammar provides a vocabulary with which one can represent a method of observing characteristic possibilities of the complex bounded by Pollock's paintings. It can state the different roles of different elements of the paintings according to rules that themselves play different roles at different times—pedagogical, analytical, paradigmatic, speculative. The grammar, however, is not a linguistic problem so much as a conceptual one; not a perceptual problem, but a philosophical one; not a phenomenology of painting, but the description of the

scene of questions. Rather than even saying a grammar is necessary prior to interpretation (and so far no one seems to know what to do with a painting per se but interpret it), the case is that the grammar comprises a separate field entirely. While the grammar indicates use, it is not use itself; it is not performative.

51. A sentence is composed of conventions, not spatial relations. Spatial relations in a sentence, like "spatial form" in the study of literature, is a metaphor for the way in which we picture the complex, as if its salient quality were the composition of effects. That is to describe a fence as made of slats *and* spatial relations rather than slats alone. In this sense a description is not a composition, meaning that a painting does not describe or depict relations of any kind, nor is it therefore a statement. A painting cannot consist of "building blocks" or layers anymore than a fence or house can be "composed." This is important to the question of a grammar insofar as painting is only metaphorically considered a layering of conventions; the conventions do not make the painting a painting, but represent themselves only. Fences and houses are only secondarily visual phenomena, even if we think some are beautiful, others ugly. Fences and houses either first of all stand or do not; the rest is a confusion of grammars.

52. One source of the inquiry into a Pollock grammar lies in the common question that roots art criticism: What does the painting mean? We ask here, on the other hand, What would constitute an explanation of the meaning of the painting? When we ask this we are wondering how it is that the meaning of a painting helps us to understand the painting or understand painting as a form of art— the actual function of art criticism. The difference between the questions can be understood by the fact that one can get the meaning of the painting wrong (unless one decides that meaning is subjective, in which case it is only a form of belief); one can misunderstand the painting. Therefore, there must be some meanings to the painting that define it as this particular one, though not all of its meanings will serve the same end. A meaning functions as a definition as well as a boundary, which we arrive at by interpret-

ing signs ("translating into [another] word-language"). How do we decide which signs possess the meanings that will lead to a definition or boundary? This is perhaps the first question on the way to explaining the meaning of meaning in the painting, a question not itself implicated in the meaning of the painting per se. But unless we can know which signs are signs of meaning, we run the risk of misreading from the outset. Another way of considering this: the use of the sign in an interpretation is not coexistent with the sign itself; and yet how the use accompanies the sign tends to seem a natural phenomena, as though signs and their use bore a natural affinity, an organicism. We grant the sign another language and so discover its use value, but we do not wonder at the mechanism by which this occurs. Even more important, we do not wonder at the fact that what we will eventually term the meaning of the painting must be in the form of sentences, indeed other kinds of sentences than those by which we determine the use of the sign. In part, then, the explanation of the meaning of the painting must engage the activities by which we move from one language to another; these activities occur as the explanation of the meaning of the meaning of the painting. The analysis of the differences between languages, between communities, constellations, requires a grammar. How are the languages structured so as to accommodate the different trails of thought? What conceptual differences create the rules of the different communities? How do such conceptual differences form the boundaries of the analyses? What are the ostensive causal connections between the languages, as well as the processes of conceptualizing not only painting in certain bounded ways but the necessary movement from one language to another? Though these are the subjects the grammar serves, the grammar is not a form of police.

53. To the extent that a grammar describes elements of correlation between language communities without conflating what Wittgenstein terms "primary" and "secondary" uses, it seeks to establish a venue for the trial of reading painting; that is, the grammar itself has a visual component, a space in which thinking finds a context, not merely a vocabulary. In part, this is the role, in the case of Pollock, of boundaries. The grammatical space

cannot be hypothetical, though the correlations made within it may be speculative. But these are known to be speculative because they do not *stand for* ostensive definitions that would lead, potentially or speculatively, to meaning. Definitions cannot be stood for whereas speculation within the grammatical space can stand for relations within the entire visual field or experience. We do not speculate on elements or definitions; we speculate on language communities.

54. If we ask, why does the meaning of a painting adhere to language, we are trying to set out a problem. A problem cannot be a muddle, though no solution is always a possibility, but this is not to say that there was no problem in the first place. Or if we say that the meaning of a painting is the feeling we have before it, then how can we talk about what it is in the painting that evokes the feeling? Why would we talk about it at all? Why should we need knowledge about painting if we did not think that painting was a kind of knowledge itself? Of what kind? That is a question for the venue of grammar.

55. The herme(neu)tics of Pollock's painting: lines that are the "same" in one context are "different" in another, in effect revising themselves as they "go along"; for example, the site of crisis on the canvas, or the visual "catastrophe," becomes in one register a transition from one hermeneutic phase to another, somewhat in the manner, allegorically speaking, of the motion of Heidegger's vocabulary within the argument of a single essay. Does this identify one way that the visual experience, the "estimating by the eye," turns into an argument? While the painting cannot itself be an argument, it can elicit a grammar of one, say about the efficacy of hermeneutics, for example. Yet it is misleading to say that a painting is a dialectic, e.g.—another inappropriate connection between metaphor and concept. Is there some way in which a painting can elicit an argument without referring us to other paintings? If the answer is no, then there is no problem. If yes, however, then it must be an effect of the grammar, which is to say the explanation of the rules by which the painting "draws" the eye; by which, in another sense, it "gazes" at the viewer.

Would we need to distinguish "a process in accordance with a rule" from "a process involving a rule"? Could it be said that the argument occurs when we at once observe the rules of the painting and then need to explain them in order to understand it? This would be, in part, like performing a calculation.

56. The matter of a logic within painting—the result of the recognition of rules—ought to be understood as a grammatical issue by which we would differentiate between effect and composition. Wittgenstein would argue that logic is a question of "can," that we calculate possibilities only in the community of "can." In an obvious sense, the experience of looking at a painting is transparent. It becomes opaque when the sign of the painting seems incomplete in itself, as it must, and the more we look at more paintings the more it does; minimalism, e.g., addresses the issue directly, though in a manner different from, say, Lichtenstein and Pop Art, whose premises include specific cultural artifacts other than themselves for even transparent understanding. The painting cannot be said to have gaps once it is presented to the viewer, and yet there is a need to fill it in, at the least by contextualizing. But context per se stands in place of the meaning of the painting, particularly when meaning appears more distant and abstract among paintings. We have seen a painting, liked it, and so want to know how it is likable; its likability seems a property of the painting. To be likable, however, indicates that we anticipate significance, and we do not long like works that elude meaning in this sense. Neither does this remain a subjective experience; meaning is indeed validated only within a community, therefore the need of context becomes a phase by which significance passes into meaning. Without necessarily questioning this passage, it becomes clear that the concept of context is a grammatical one because while we can say that a painting is a sign (and therefore significant), we cannot say that meaning accompanies the sign anymore than writing accompanies thinking.

57. What kinds of sentences are possibly meaningful in the face of the "inexactness" of the signs that comprise painting when we

understand that the signs are the display of rules and the rules, like the lines in Pollock, are usable and can be obeyed in more than one direction? A grammar that would elicit possibly meaningful sentences must schematize, even tentatively, the various directions the signs point to. Nor would this reflect a gap in the grammar or the painting, but in fact a precision, an exactness that treats inexactness. This is the way in which we mean the logic of the painting; not only what we can account for but what we must account for rather than resorting to the traditional readings that leap over such problems in order to arrive at an essence, a truth (even Benjamin's "intentionlessness of truth") that transcends the question of how we can explain the statements we make about painting. The ideal, let us say, lies in the painting, not in the vagueness, irrelevance or disorder of what we say about it. Clarity is not the result of interpretation, but the requirement for it.

58. It is possible that abstraction has reduced the issue of the painterly by replacing a picture of things in the world with the method of picturing. Perhaps this is why the symbology attached to abstraction has tended toward the mythic and metaphysical dimensions of the unconscious when in fact the notion of "painting" the unconscious is a misleading way to speak of displacing representation. Just as surrealism tended toward the mechanistic in its treatment of mind, so too does the unconscious "imagery" of abstraction seem more formulaically morphic than an effort to "represent" the mind, spirit, etc. The absence of a specific grammar for abstraction has led to the acceptance of, say, the unconscious in Pollock as the signature of his paintings. This, of course, directs the paintings to the language communities that have treated them: psychoanalytic, mythic, historiographic (how has the unconscious emerged in other and previous painters?), technical (how does the use, e.g., of debris represent the surfacing of the unconscious?)—how these represent mind, the trace of them in the "development" of his painting (as though the unconscious, say, underwent concomitant "development"). Within such models of systematic thought, which literally bring the paintings *inside,* what is the distinction between rules of the paintings and rules of the model by which the paintings are seen

as either inside or outside, relevant or not relevant to the means by which meanings can be ascribed, or rather must be ascribed? While it is not a question of the arbitrariness of models per se, we can question the arbitrary choice of certain limits within which a model appears more appropriate than another, and surely more appropriate than no model at all.

59. The abstract painting, an object both different from and similar to other objects, including other paintings, bewilders us to the extent that rather than seeing a representation of the world (reading the painting as "signing" things in the world), we "image" something, often an idea, sometimes an emotion. Two things: (1) the image is different from the painting and (2) the space in which we image—in effect abstracting from the abstraction in order to bring the painting inside—is different from that space in which we interpret the painting. Imaging, then, is no longer the act of seeing; that is, it is already an act of displacement or appropriation for the purpose of understanding. One could say this recognizes that the purest visual field for imaging is a completely dark room. Perhaps such an image best represents the site in which grammar becomes necessary. What is more, imaging (the opening of the possibility of taking the painting inside) does not itself form only a picture, but the road of translation to language. Language is the interpreter; seeing has been left behind.

60. Though we can readily understand how sentences become pictures in the mind, and how pictures (examples, analogies, etc.) aid in the understanding of abstractions, what happens when pictures become sentences, without which pictures cannot be said to mean? Are we applying the picture to constructions of language already available? Does the picture supply us with a representation seemingly less mediated by signs than the language itself?—this would be a psychological rather than philosophical process, and not necessarily accurate. What sorts of meaning are valid within the mechanism by which pictures become sentences? How often does description limit the possibilities of meaning (in the manner of Sartre's stroll through a garden

that becomes in his mind a rose garden because he has seen roses in it)? How are descriptions framed by: (1) the desire to implant a picture in the mind of another, (2) the tradition, genre, etc., to which we attribute determining features of the painting, (3) the context in which we understand the tradition, genre, etc., as living in the present? Does meaning dis-integrate the painting for the purpose of yielding up a solution to the reading of signs *qua* signs? Can a painting, at this register, ever mislead, be misread, or not make sense? Would it be a failure of the painting or of language if it did? Can its meaning "deepen" to the extent that in another epoch a paradigm and grammar may appear more "appropriate" to explaining the painting, as today Velázquez and Vermeer seem to be "significant" to theory. Or, when we come to value a painter previously undervalued, is it because we have learned to be better readers or because we have sentences we earlier lacked?

61. To say that the description of a painting "approximates" or "translates" what the surface of a canvas contains or evokes is to say that the description orients us by a linguistic *appearance,* itself misleading insofar as the description slides between metaphor, reality and feeling in the realm, psychologically or philosophically, of "as if." The process of interpretation always begins with such a description, limited only by all the possible sentences we could utter in the realm of "as if." Wittgenstein: "This is like some sentence, but what sentence is it like?" (*Lectures on Aesthetics,* 19). The description of a painting offers similar possibilities of sifting through sentences that approximate the painting or the sensation of seeing the painting. This becomes the scene of writing for grammar which surveys the misleading linguistic appearances that provide the vocabulary of interpretation. The description exists then, but as a false step. Or, what is the categorical difference between painting as sign and language as sign as we only understand the former by the latter? In a sense, when we view a painting, we do not think so much as model an image that becomes the object of our thought. Thinking on that object is a methodological search in that we are learning to perfect ways of combining or associating images with linguistic representations

of them. One might say, for example, that there are so many associations between Pollock's paintings and *Finnegans Wake* (including a possible "influence") that a Pollock grammar might consist of Joycean descriptions, or that Shem the Penman could represent the paintings more aptly within his sign system than we can in ours: "allalluvial," "chronic spinosis," "traumway," "sexophonolinguistic schizophrenesis," etc. This makes more sense of the paintings than other forms of subtler indebtedness without, necessarily, being an analogy. We would say this is what the methodological search consists of.

62. A particular meaning must reside in Pollock's paintings because we have learned to translate so-and-so into this-and-that. This is how significance has been bestowed on the paintings, and it serves therefore as the point of departure for thinking the possibility of a grammar. Because the sign system of the paintings is unfamiliar, tradition has it that the application of a familiar mode of analysis will provide an order that renders it intelligible. In order to avoid an analysis based on subtracting from representation or the history of representation, the reader of the paintings brings them into a language community that first of all presumes to be able to describe not only reading painting but writing the thinking about reading painting. The acquisition of the paintings takes place when not enough of our known visual grammar indicates the presence of painting; this process accounts for the opening up of painting to the point where we can safely ask today, What other kinds of objects can be considered paintings? The concept of painting in Pollock is the first, or at least foremost, to radicalize the language of visual impression without being parodic; in a sense, the reader of Pollock has always wondered what Pollock put in place of centers, frames, perspectives, morphs, etc., in order to yet establish that the work was painting. And if it was, what were those elements doing in painting before other than arbitrarily occupying space and subverting the languages used to analyze them?

63.   Can we say that a difference between visual impression and interpretation lies, in the case of Pollock, for example, in the

involuntary and voluntary tracing of lines? If so, the former would be intentionless, the latter intended, in effect intended for interpretation. Which of these might provoke us to say, "That is probably a painting," and which "That looks like a painting?" The two statements are infused by different states, or even different ways, of reading painting: the first is not only expressing uncertainty but disillusionment; the second bears the experience of prior description. One need not have ever seen a painting to utter the former, but to utter the latter one might have seen one or one thousand paintings. The point is that while the visual impression is closer to uncertainty than interpretation, interpretation dismisses that phase of the road to understanding. In a sense, then, interpretation overcomes disillusionment; or interpretation is itself illusionment (enchantment). Interpretation cannot proceed without the belief that the sign is meaningful, is meant, is intended (for me). But how are lines and colors intended for me? This edges dangerously close to problem-solving as redemption, as a paranoia-criticism in which the boundaries of signs are known by the mystery of conscious, or even unconscious, projection.

64. Visual impression, in fact, depends upon looking, while the imaging that takes place for interpretation depends upon not looking, or on looking with an eye toward concept, a willed and therefore linguistic experience. The imaging relies not only on the memory of other paintings, but of linguistic structures that serve to conceptualize—here is the emergence of certainty that replaces disillusionment. Perhaps it is the path to certainty that we remember when we look at a painting. As with what it is that the painting as a sign "knows," the issue is one of framing; to this extent the formalism that enables the frame to frame is as much ornamental as rational, but the value of it as ornament is only useful to the degree to which it is also rational.

65. Though everyone experiences some sensation in the presence of a painting, many conclude that the meaning of the painting is being kept a secret, even a hostage to knowledge. Is this like being able to use certain words without knowing their pre-

cise definitions? Or that their definitions become confused, say, with the sound of them, as though by their sound they ought to mean something other than they do? Does this suggest that sensations pose questions so that the activity of analysis would really be an effort to explain why we experience what we feel in the presence of this or that painting? But this would be a trivial goal in comparison to the sensation itself (like deciding that the analysis of sexual passion is the genuine purpose of feeling it), and would only be of value to a poetics of effect. What is the connection between meaning and knowledge if knowledge is not the translation of something prior to its expression, to our awareness of it; and meaning, we feel, is imbedded in the object or in our relationship to it in ways indifferent to our knowledge?

66. A visual impression, the two-way road of cause and effect, constitutes horizon insofar as it unifies the painting, putting line and line together, color and color, color and line, etc. Putting together is the rehearsed activity that "sees this as that," that familiarizes the order of signs and prefigures linguistic action. But it also puts together in the paradoxical mode of not unifying: when these parts are put together, they are not a whole. To go beyond this is to move from the concept of seeing to the theory in which the paradox occupies a position in the understanding of the painting and the creation of a grammar for it. Even if the absence of unity when the parts are put together could be said to constitute a description (and not just an assumption or judgment), we would still be able to understand the painting as meaningful while pursuing the question of the relationship between meaning and unity—not that it still must be meaningful, but that it could be. Yet the analysis of painting, particularly of abstraction, dismisses or neglects both the issue and the painting. Here Wittgenstein, for example, would reply that only intended paintings can be meaningful because intention provides the threshold of interpretation, an axiom that continues to haunt analysis in the guises of reader-response and, more subtly, intertextuality. The intention, as the element that defies further interpretation, is the visual impression itself (psychologically speaking) in that one does not think a visual impression anymore

than one thinks a dream. The painting is only something other than visual impression when it is isolated from the intention that by definition is not interpretable. Afterward one must always be clear whether the method is applied to the painting or the painting to the method. In one sense the question is: Are there certain paintings that we cannot learn to read? Whether we apply correlations based on "and so on," "this and that," "instead of," etc., how a certain painting is a painting can neither be described nor explained? Unreadability, in its variant guises, would have to occupy a space in grammar equal to the various modes of readability, and not as an opposition since unreadability and readability remain on the same path to knowledge.

67. On that same path of encoded doubt flowered at once by readability and unreadability, *Finnegans Wake*'s "chronic spinosis" is not only the result of copula (the biblical "ands" that beget) but its apparent contradictory "or" that makes language simultaneously continue and halt. The relation between "and" and "or" in the reading requirement establishes a serialist model of conflict and continuity. Learning to read the *Wake* requires mastery not of language per se but of apprehending misapprehension as a rule of the game. The "abnihilisation of the etym" (*etymos* as both origin and truth) means that the digressive style of grafting and "logokleptism" makes referral and deferral the positions on the chessboard of the game: the slippage of knowledge is the knowledge the book offers. In contradiction to the hokey mythifications (the consequence of copula in the *Wake*) that critics who would "familiarize" the book elaborate, the "or" of doubt displaces story by encyclopedic rhetorism.

68. "Whorled without end": in the overlain skeins of the riverrun (*reverons,* riverain) that mediate Joyce and Pollock, there are, literally, no margins for error. What is error when there is no synthesis, no destination? In this sense Joyce takes the unconscious as literally as Kafka did Freud, meaning he borrows the language game without its analysis. And here unconsciousness stands for the indeterminacy of the overdetermined, the simultaneous surfeit and dearth of the meaning of dream, for example.

To paraphrase Lyotard, identity is the victim of excess and, since identity establishes itself in adhering to a unity, its absence leads beyond loss, failure, etc. What Joyce and Pollock's works require then is to be looked at theoretically, in the sense that *theoria* means looking without nostalgia; this is why, in literal terms, theory is speculative, not normative. In theory, as in Pollock and the *Wake,* there are no subject-object relations, because, while there is a subject of the postmodern variety, there is no concept ego. Rules of representation, and the history of those rules, are bound by the concept ego to the extent that ego is either wrongfully identified with subject or, more pertinently, stands in relation to otherness in a more psycho-philosophically complex way than the self-representing (self-signing is more precise) subject. If, to the auto-lisible subject, there is an object of knowledge, it is *theoria* itself in its specular register, in its "ipseity."

69. If the reader of a Pollock painting said that the artist was recording "sense-data," we would not easily know if that were a statement concerning grammar or an assertion that Pollock invented a new way of painting perhaps reflecting a certain argument in analytic philosophy. We would need to know if this were a statement of a visual impression or of interpretation (in this case, analogy). Why should such a distinction matter? Because without it, we would not be able to know whether the reader understands the painting or is describing a sensation; that is, whether the painting can be meaning something or if, in fact, the reader is making a grammatical remark only. In a sense, then, there is a categorical difference between an argument concerning the painting and one concerning forms of argument, a difference which, without a grammar, would otherwise continue to be hidden. By describing the grammar, one describes how a line of thought can or cannot be an analysis; we can understand what is still not meaningful, but we cannot arrive at meaning without understanding, including such relationships as those among linguistic communities ("A rose is still red in the dark"). In the case of painting, and of Pollock as example, the problem remains a familiar one: if you are painting, aren't you painting *something*? Even when the analysis of abstract art pretends not to address

this question, it does so by using the conceptual structures of representational art analysis, historicism, etc., as if, for instance, a continuity of either works or analyses were given; as if paintings were born into them. The trouble with paraphrase—what analysis employs as evidence of the painting's presence—is that while we may understand by it elements common to other paintings or other analyses, we cannot know how whatever the painting means could not be meant by other paintings. This is not an issue of originality or novelty, but of identity.

70. The verb *to be* indicates the two meanings of equation and copula, separate states of affairs comprised, potentially, of the same elements when applied not to language (where the elements must be different) but to painting. Example: the lines in Pollock equal each other; the lines in Pollock are added to each other. This is not a way to characterize the function of the lines, though we could make such a case, but to characterize the identity of the lines, or to characterize the way in which the lines do not offer a single sign, though they are a single aspect of the painting. By tracing the path of the drawn grammar of the line, we learn the language by which lines can be purposive. So we would consider the lines in equality and as added to one another, and relate these findings to each other as the identity of the line as sign in the sign system. The status of the line, then, is variously expectant, multiplicitously transitive. When we learn the rules of analysis by examples and paradigms, how much expectation do we delimit? And why do we delimit as a way of *materializing* the "impalpable"? Communities of thought exist by not recognizing there may be more questions to pose.

71. A problem regarding the identity of lines in Pollock: we find that a painting appears either flat or three-dimensional depending on whether lines intersect or overlap, and whether the "ground" is constant or changes color, texture, etc. A consequence of this for analysis is the perennial search for cause (i.e., tradition, optics) when it is, in fact, a conceptual matter whether lines penetrate each other, stop and start, or collide. In any of the cases, could one reading be more descriptive than another, and, if so, more genu-

ine? And would the others, if not all of them, be seeing the lines in the mode of "as if"? To pose the more difficult question, what would constitute ground in such a painting, or in such a grammar (though the presumption of a ground in Pollock is standard)? This might be like the question of whether stars are set against the sky or cut out of it—a conundrum of visual impressionism that presumes we see objects when in fact we see only the arrows that objects were once somewhere else; in painterly terms, whether we find shapes because of color or vice versa. We see the painting framed differently, meaning we see it hypothetically.

72. In Pollock's paintings, the vanishing point unavailable to the eye resides at the intersect of the visual experience and the sign. Because we cannot measure how we *see* Pollock's paintings, we measure instead how his paintings see us not measuring them— that metaphorical dialectic of desire in the lower register of absence. The trouble is that if the paintings are contingent in this manner, what are we to say of the reader's desire? This question has been viewed as ontological, psychological, but not as a question of grammar.

73. Just as a painting has no identity until it is brought into the history of painting, the history of painting must be returned to the theory of which it is a paradigm of linguistic community. Art histories are examples of theories of cognition, and in that sense all art history has been commentary on the status of representation. Theory is always the elaboration of a cultural stubbornness concerning things in the world and how we determine their value.

74. The effort to return theory to history, to implicate history (and the history of theory) in theory must take many forms, some analogous to finding and un-finding the history of representation implicated in abstract art. If I say that these fragments— some of which imitate the propositional logic of Wittgenstein, some of which negate the possibility of Wittgenstein's contribution to the discussion (and by that would draw a picture of the modernist fragment for postmodernism)—by their internal motion, their strategic placement, the structure of them in discrete

groupings, already return theory and history into relations identifiable before Pollock painted and Wittgenstein wrote, I am signaling to myself how history is embedded in discourse. We are in touch here with three principles regarding the fragment and history: one, the "romanticism" of the fragment (Nancy and Lacoue-Labarthe); two, Benjamin's shards that cannot be identified as a "shattered bowl"; three, Blanchot's fragments whose meaning is determined by the totality after which they appear. (As such, the Eternal in Eternal Return is not Eternal, but it is a return.) The "I say" of these fragments is, as "Blanchot says," only a "canonical abbreviation for a rule of identity." What of this observation in relation to the paintings not yet identified except as "Pollock's" other than that the displaced "I" is already the displaced "Pollock" of the statements his paintings constitute (the speech that "statement" stands for); and that these displacements are the hypothetical Is of the same that the I of writing is.

75. Without saying that in language, as in painting, anything can be understood as anything else (note here the dialogue between Wittgenstein's boundaries to the language of a proposition and Benjamin's theory of allegory), we might assume that signs point and arguments tell us to what they point; however, their structural features differ in such a way that there is a something mediating sign and argument, itself structured differently again, its effect and appeal those of another linguistic community. In some sense, we refer to mediators as bridges, but that, in this case, provides the wrong image, as though the mediator touched both sign and argument, as though the mediator were composed, in part, by some feature of sign and of argument. Most important, however, this would mean that argument itself could not be a sign. If we extend the thought of this to the function of rhetoric in both sign and argument, we can view subjectivity as a trope, sufficiently contingent that it would be known as a position only (Wittgenstein's chessboard) and not as a thing occupying a position. Does this suggest the exhaustion of a grammar of sign and argument? Could we suggest exhaustion without rhetorical devices?

76. "No sign leads us beyond itself, and no argument either" (*Philosophical Grammar,* 114).

77. With regard to painting, though Wittgenstein applies it generally, one reason "there is no such thing as a completed grammar" returns us to the problem of sensation. Sensation is neither a faculty of the mind nor antecedent to any presumptions about a mental effect because of it. The special sense of sensation with regard to painting is generally not acknowledged as such; that is the first error interpretation makes. The second is that there can be no special sense of sensation that would not mistakenly confuse language communities even in the manner of Russell's theory of descriptions, which, while problematic within art, accounts for the difference between perception and sensation. Completed grammar is here impossible because when the reader of a painting describes a sensation, not only is sensation a misplaced concept but so is description. If in fact I am naming a sensation, I have already precluded describing insofar as naming is a point and describing points toward. What one sees by this example is, at the least, the hidden necessity of the incompleteness of grammar in the face of vocabularies that confuse points with arrows so to speak, or states with processes. It is perhaps the residue of the aesthetics of copula, of the painting as an *is.*

78. On the incompleteness of a Pollock grammar: lines that do not provide borders, grounds that are neither fore nor back, destinations that are not frames—all these, at once descriptions and contradistinctions, are rules of Pollock paintings. The usage of these rules constitutes the syntax of the paintings; in the precise sense that syntax and semantics are indistinguishable within Wittgenstein's grammar, the incompleteness lies within the fact therefore that there can be no distinction between the paintings as "sensible non-sense" and "nonsense," the concealed point of departure for the analysis of abstract art. In brief, a painting with lines and no frame is still a painting—that is one way of expressing the necessary incompleteness.

79. The rules are transparent, consistent, expressible, but we do not know what validates them or what they validate. There may be mystery at the source, but it should not be false mystery; what paradigm, for example, enables these rules to be derived from it?

If, in fact, they are said meanwhile to validate mystery while not being derived from it, then there could be nothing stated about the paintings as objects. If this is the case, then how could there be said to be paintings at all? If a maxim of misrule provided the theory for the paintings, then we would be looking at disguised nonsense, in which case anything said about them would be said about nonproblems. But problems can be proposed, so that is not the case. In short, the identity of the paintings as paintings is problematic, not nonproblematic in any sense.

80. The additional problem in the role of "sensation" lies in its relationship to the concept understanding. Sensations do not accompany the meanings of sentences, unless we choose to use sensation in a strict metaphoric sense or expand meaning to include musical qualities we may attribute to language. Understanding concerns obedience to rules, recognition of the orders of forms; this is why we can explain rules but not understanding itself. If we try to relate sensation to understanding, we will of course note not only different orders of forms but different categories of experience within which the rules are inscribed. Any discussion of the relationship, however, must be accompanied by the caution that what is being constructed is an essentialist evolutionary paradigm for our consciousness of art objects. What is useful from Wittgenstein in this dilemma—again a concealed copula in the tradition of writing about art—is that mastering the rules of relations (what is known as "going on in the same way") constitutes the model whereby the painting becomes identical with itself. It is as if the work is now open to analysis instead of debate about its status; it is analyzable within tradition only when it is unequivocally a painting. We would be wiser to ask if sensation and intuition are synonyms once rules of understanding have been established. And if we say that intuition in fact offers the true basis for understanding painting, then we are left with the dilemma of what is being understood. Intuitions about reading paintings may be as misleading as intuitions about how houses are built or how autos run. When intuitions are not misleading, however, they stipulate something, which means that they are no longer intuitions; in this

sense one can learn as well as invent, but one cannot discover the meaning of a painting.

81. Within the collision of sensation, intuition and understanding, it is less a problem that material and figural readings are at odds with each other than that they must be viewed as, respectively, intrinsic and extrinsic to the painting. The dichotomous relations of inside and outside reflect a tradition of thinking into being the object's "natural" integrity, a tradition at once challenged by the "flatness" of modernist works (including, I would note, the "superficiality" of acrylics) and more recently the exposure of oppositional thinking to the scrutiny of poststructuralism. The prefoundational organic or syncretic assumptions of the status of the object for interpretation inevitably leads to establishing boundaries between the authenticity of the work of art (unbounded by time, universally meaningful) and the cultural demands that reading a painting reflects. While this would seem a boundary no longer efficacious, or at least in disrepute, it is implicit in the homogenizing of cultural criticism, semiotics and speech-act theory, most often observed in the "appropriation" of postformalist methods for the purpose of quasi-political theories of culture. What is the difference, that is to say, between "looking *at* a painting" and "looking *into* a mirror"? To paraphrase Wittgenstein, if I own a mirror, do I own the reflection in it? And, not paraphrasing, is my reflection of myself a "representation" of me to another person also seeing my reflection in the mirror?

82. If I say that I can only understand any painting by understanding a Pollock painting—on the face of it absurd—I am in fact reversing the basic paradigm of theories of art history and criticism. While no one would say that the history of painting constitutes a *series* per se, the intuition by which paintings are located in order to provide cohesion suggests this. As a psychopedagogical "decision," the need for homogeneity determines the "insights," "meanings" and "recognitions" by which tradition can at once "slip" to accommodate the new and remain tradition. Tradition is not, in effect, *a* tradition or a discrete set of traditions (pedagogical specializations) but a process whereby correspon-

dences, influences, even so-called revolutions occur within the same locus. While there may be differing models for the reading of painting (religious, mythic, societal, painterly), there remains at the least a residue of a notion of *development* in the continuities within and between them. Whether one knows how to "continue the thinking" becomes the basis for valuing a particular perspective. In this sense, though, the history is always a progression in the guise of primordial aesthetic drama—the individuality of the artist who, while not creating out of a void, retains an originary authority even if we are uncertain if he or she creates from "chaos" or from tradition. It is as though the integrity of the art object can only be maintained if it is a fundamentally ur-historical object; or, as in the case of concept art (Pop and post-Pop), if the ephemerality of the object can be justified within a larger cultural invention (i.e., postmodernity). Specific meaning would seem to be put into the object only if it already possesses an intuited one from art history's developmental or evolutionary scheme. This is not, however, the same as saying that art is only the art which tells us what we already know, but rather what we already could calculate as knowable.

83. Whether art reading informs "this painting means this" or "Pollock intended this" or "the painting works like this," it is because we understand a language in which the experience of the painting is less important than instructions; that is, meaning, intention and even process do not have the psychological sources we grant them, but instead the one source of being reiterable. This is why there is never for very long a "special case" in the history of painting. Rather than nothing really "odd" being able to survive, nothing remains odd; there is not a "false" painting, for example (here we might pursue the corrections that reread and revalued El Greco and certain works of Degas and Monet that were either "flawed" or explained by the artists' ocular difficulties). The "thisness" of painting outruns thinking on behalf of a reiteration whose consequences negate, in many instances, the very signs that "thisness" can point toward. Deduction is traceable here as a technique by which the *this*ness (the painting as a predicate to the rules of interpretation) appears to

be established. In fact, however, it is usually the case that the practice is normative: not a reading according to rules established by a painting but by putative judgments as to where meaning resides and how reading can "recover" it.

84. The principal framework, then, in which reading a painting occurs is noncontradiction. If there were not already an agreement that marks in paint on a canvas constituted an arguable painting, we would have to invent another measure for what a painting might be; for example, only marks in red, yellow and blue signify the presence of art, while those in black or white might provide a site in which a painting might be found, but not necessarily. Worse, we would have to invent a measure for what a painting is not. While this seems absurd, or contradictory to experience, it points to a distinction between a state of affairs and the characterization of one as painting, or for language as describing painting. For example, what is the relationship of white in the history of painting to Robert Ryman's white paintings? In a sense the absence of color on canvas is already framed; because it is already a painting (of the sort that makes us read hues of white and brushstrokes in a special way), or specifically *already a painting now in our culture* it is meaningful, so that white and brushstrokes resonately circumscribe and inform Rymans in ways categorically different from Vermeers, say. What, then, is "sempiternal" about the framework of the institution that can characterize whiteness as such? (My cat, if I had one, might want to lie in the sunshine on even a cloudy day, but it would not want to see Paris.)

85. That comparison is the experiential model for the analysis of painting means that there exist representations of relations between concepts which, because viewed as synthetic, are misleading. Appearing as descriptions of necessary relations within a painting, such representations of conceptual "dynamics" in fact reiterate the boundaries of possible meanings for certain statements about works. That is to say, what analysis terms necessary relations within a painting are normative statements concerning rules of representation. This would be less an issue were it not

for the fact that almost no art analysis occurs without a confusion that results in the misdirection of "recovering" essences out of a quasi-perceptual psychology: telling us what we see, how it happens that we see that, and what the effect therefore is on the history of art and/or art reading. At once a false collaboration between psychologism and decisions of art-historical judgment, this ruse drives toward not only the collapse of modes of discourse into statements of ostensible knowledge, but is moreover the signpost of the principle that in the name of the object descriptions of comparative relations ("dynamics," for example) are projected onto it. Indeed, the term dynamics, which haunts art reading, like dialectics, the way drunks haunt lampposts, proclaims an artificial distance between the object and the "rules of representation" which supplies the basis for concealing in actuality the expression of stipulated relations within the painting. The point is that such a romanticism, pervasive as it is, is not just the goal or result of certain techniques but is the institution itself; only a totalizing practice can indicate when a "void" either exists or can be filled, so that, for example, fragmentation is always of a totality against which to be measured. The ratio of meaning remains a concealed contract between how we read and how we enunciate. In one regard a fault lies in the primacy of a psychology of perception, as if color and line were, for instance, *essentially* matters of sense perception, as opposed, let us say, to a philosophy of perception, or even a politics of it. Similar to erroneous understandings of logical impossibility, the institutional practice would have it that it is not a matter in reality of agreements on ways of speaking but on provable perceptions of the object, a pseudoscientific model connecting how we see to knowledge of objects, as if concepts of dynamism, dialexis or arthistorical tradition itself were mediators rather than axioms that, of course, cannot be proven wrong.

86. Can we say that the significance of a painting is determined by other paintings in which similar properties unfold as if in a series so that we can distinguish what is essential from what is nonessential? Can we say, either alternatively or additionally, that the significance of a painting (its validation by writing of it) is

determined by its capacity for appropriation into art-historical categories in a manner similar to the previous question? What is the relationship between the two? We would be recognizing rules by the reappearance of features that would have to be determined as internal guarantors of, at the least, a historical site within the normative locus theories of art constitute. This would mean that norms of representation (ostensibly within the painting, but certainly within the theories) depend upon at first being surprised by a "discovery" (whether of new or older work— "rediscovered") only to prove that by *finding transitions* among series of essentials we can understand how the painting should not have surprised us. At such a point, however, we would be hard pressed to say what it was in our reading that we might have expected *not* to be the case about the painting; that is, what was in the painting to disprove? Validation through interdependency is the reason why art reading cannot see validity as an invention, does not recognize that the arbitrariness of its techniques ensures that there will have been no gaps between paintings. Ascribing significance then is art reading's invention of its own locus and persists as an explanation of the extended system, which includes theory, history, criticism, archival research, as well as art journalism, curating, and collecting. In a sense, nothing can fail to be resolved because, contrary to the normative view, the art reader begins already understanding what is being invented without knowing it as invention. In effect, the analysis is itself the result; the painting does not have to be looked for, indeed it *cannot* be looked for. All techniques have already been found or there would be nothing to say. If we say that Pollock invented a new use for the line in painting by a technique of multiplication, it is the rules of multiplication that are the grammar, not the effect of the multiplication, not the object the painting. The effect closes the gap between the technique and the use of it in abstract art, as if, for example, the twelve-tone scale already signified music, or as if inventing a series already meant correct calculation.

87. Question: What sorts of statements can writing about abstract art make when concepts underlying characterizations of

spatial relations on canvas originate as representations of how we see the real world? Literally, the writing must abstract from those concepts so that, for example, "nonobjective" connotes a loss of the external world and traces an inward development in the history of painting, that is, the evolution of expressionism. It is as though the concept of representation were attached to realism simply because painting is a visual experience. Is this why there is so much said about states of being and the material conditions of painting? Or, in contrast, renewable efforts to read paintings as cultural artifacts before they are read as paintings? That is, the language of abstract art reading specifically seems still to depend upon either subtraction or substitution, which themselves, of course, can form the basis for cultural criticism, but that requires another grammar entirely. As it is, the analyses of internal relations on canvas have not abandoned their realist origins and so can only "recover" or "discover" representation or nonrepresentation. Most of all, abstract art reading has returned us to the most primitive notions of how abstraction can represent; namely, the bio-morphism of what shapes "look like" and how colors "evoke" feelings—consider Pollocks as landscapes, Rothkos as prayers. Is this how such paintings compel us? Is this what they compel us toward? Can we say that we tend to write about paintings whose boundaries seem certain to us even though we can only locate the certainty within a technique whereby looking actually follows interpretation? Which would mean that it isn't certainty itself compelling us as that the urge to interpret requires us to exclude doubt at the outset in order to express the transformation of the visual experience into a cultural determination.

88. Toward a new concept of representation in painting? Focus first on the "aboutness" that underlies not only descriptions of paintings but the proximity of critical language to the ideal objects that experiencing paintings as "universals" makes of them. Rather than understanding Pollocks, for example, as expressing ideas in the imagination, in a "realm" where true statements exist but are not represented, we can state that the paintings represent unlimited methods of multiplication; on the one hand we do not

restrict the paintings to imitations of each other, decomposition of other painters' paintings or expressions of some paradisiacal or infernal region where "abstract objects" could be said to exist (a Euclidean world, for example). Instead of choosing between theories of space into which Pollocks might fit as abstract expressions, or between theories of space/time by which "relations" can be accounted for, if we consider *exactitude* as a grammatical feature, then our descriptions and statements concerning space or space and time occur within a paradigm of rules of reason that are, grammatically speaking, also rules of representation. An analogy would be the notation system and its uses as the exactitudes of musical composition. We want to answer the question: How is painting representation if it does not correspond to reality or models of reading reality; and if it is not representation, then how is it not tautological? That is, how can we say anything concerning painting that makes sense; that is to say, that can separate sense from non-sense? Norms for describing paintings, which form the basis for all interpretations and archival studies, license a language of conformation, understanding by inference; or a specific convention that is *a priori* certain of the conditions by which paintings compel us. This is a belief system without gods but with hierarchies. "Aboutness" in fact takes certainty as its point of departure, as if "about" can be a model of semantics. In a field in which we are convinced by an argument because it corresponds to what we have already inferred, what constitutes understanding are wishes, which do not even have the force of dreams.

89. Insofar as paintings retain the trace of being "statements," their treatment transforms them into forms of expression that ought to be recognizable by reasonable readers without at the same time actually constituting sentences. In this regard there is a fundamental confusion between the enunciation of a grammar and the role of a grammar in the understanding of painting. The reason that painting must say something about the world is that reading a painting aspires to know something about the world and wishes to retain the painting as something truer than an occasion. Such a reduction as this statement simply describes the

problem that results from intending contingent relations to be necessary, as if choosing among possible responses to a painting makes that into not only a property of the painting, but *our* property.

90. Reading a painting begins with a gaze that absorbs the whole; in this sense our first acquaintance is a timeless experience of spatial relations. It is as we want to know what the painting signifies that we invent time for it. Picturing cannot be interpreted without being subjected to time; only in the context of time then is something true or false, or sense or non-sense. As in Marin's study of Poussin, where historical painting is characterized as "time intelligibility in a spatial medium," art reading uses time to make spatial relations of the gaze meaningful; that is to say, the narrative proposition (locus, according to Marin) of historical painting (the before and after that implicates metaphysics in the interpretation) already invents the theoretical position of art writing in general. Just as painting can lead us to admire things in the world we otherwise would not by a process of transforming juxtaposition into displacement (the intention of the gaze in the face of spatial relations), so art reading reveals its debt to metaphysics when, in the name of problem solving and giving meaning, it moves visual signs into linguistic loci. At one register, the effect of this is to obfuscate the distinction between paintings that "need" us (Poussin, Vermeer) and those that do not (Pollock). To reveal the distinction, however, would be to acknowledge that art exists which may be semantically ineffable. Understand that in the arena of language and logic, this difficulty led Wittgenstein to the proposition that syntax and semantics were the same ("scaffolding is the meaning"). It is by the identification of syntax and semantics that Wittgenstein avoids the accusation of formalism.

91. Language disguises the thought of metaphysics that adheres to statements about the meanings of paintings. Not only are paintings semantic mysteries but impersonal ones. As this study is a locus of instruction in a method toward objects that do not need it in order to exist in their fullness, so are the paintings of Pollock

themselves. Because, however, this instruction and that of Pollock are conceptually different, it is possible to address the paintings without reading any one of them below the level of a grammatical theory; a coda, however, would be interpretive by view of enlisting a coda at all.

92. When I propose that modernist thinking is an effort to actualize hypothetical thinking in three distinct modes, I am suggesting that the dominant language games are mythic, tautological and hermeneutical, all of which share the figure of "horizon" as points of departure and termination, and have their effects by virtue of the concept "as if" (in which correspondence theory turns into a theory of representation). Mythic thought is the circular appropriation or exclusion of reason and chance into or from the model; tautology is the chiastic model of a mirroring function or intention; hermeneutics is the widening or narrowing spiral that deliberately comprehends its metaphorical language as the origin of rational investigation (in this it manages to critique metaphysics without, however, questioning the category of Being, itself a metaphysical proposition). These scaffolds have determined the course of modern art theory: circle, chiasm, spiral. The methods that once seemed efficacious have resulted in placing the art object itself (the impersonal semantic mystery) in a black hole, or to be more precise, have understood the impersonal semantic mystery as a black hole. Pollock's paintings, like *Finnegans Wake* in literature, are the big bangs of the postmodern.

93. The momentary fulfillment of seeing a Pollock painting is not only already the trace of the painter's anticipatory utopia that abstraction constitutes but, equally, the arrow that indicates the ruins of utopia. Dream, myth, psychoanalysis, the "representation" of nature—categories of appropriation which tell us that in the painting lies the trace not of fulfillment per se but the recognition that the moment for the possibility of fulfillment has already been lost. The domestic materials of the paintings do not point to a future, to the not-yet-in-existence of the avant-garde but to the wish that the *exposé* of the real were commensurate

with it. Similarly, the avowed "intimacy" of the paintings is questioned by their scale—walls without museums at one register, while at another murals that could not long last in a personal space and indeed point toward unframed paintings in museums (one of Pollock's achievements with respect to the measurement of significant art).

94. What would be elicited by the application of catastrophe theory to Pollock's paintings? Recognize first that Thom's morphologies reiterate the "looks" of Pollock's lines, specifically in those known as reject ($\vee$), cross ($\setminus$), shake ($\wedge$), give ($\diagup$), send ($\times$), and cut off (λ). This is not to say that all the morphologies do not appear, they do, but that these (and especially the "umbilics") present the cognitive scene of the paintings as hypotheses. Particularly if we read Pollock in light of Thom's second principle that catastrophes along a simple path are semantic, resulting from verbs expressing action, change and event, we can at least indicate the behavior of line from a theory of destabilization. The leap would be, of course, an analysis according to the optical effects of the specific morphologies as a sign system. Meanwhile they can provide a vocabulary that schematizes what the canvases prize and what they do not, e.g. being ($-$). We might also suggest that what is indicated by the instability of Pollock's basic morphologies is the presentation, in Thom's archetypes, of nonexistence. We could trace as well in the instrumental interpretation the nature of body movement during the act of painting. There are in both measurements of space and time to account for birth, life, and death within a specific area as a line enters, appears, and exits, suggesting transience as well as instants of being *inside.* Where each domain is represented in the scheme by a rectangle, the analysis of line within it (in which, e.g., so-called accentuations ["lips" $\langle\rangle$ in the schema] can indicate the frequency and type of catastrophe. In addition, attraction and aversion to color could be schematized by the analysis of luminosity. This would constitute an imminent criticism of the paintings by virtue of the "archetypal" grammar Thom employs, one that in the face of myth itself would seem to intend to ally myth, nature and mathematics (a

Pythagoreanism for the postmodern?), but might also in fact create a new collision among them.

95. While one effect of a grammar of abstraction is demystification, that is not a primary function of it insofar as demystification historically partakes of a "truth-telling" reserved for ideological debate. Rooted in historical circumstances, demystification inevitably draws its boundaries at the politico-cultural needs of a limited period of time. Grammar, on the other hand, is limited, as it is marked, by linguistic possibilities that in other contexts and in other uses might provide modes of demystification a strategy but not a cause *sui generis.* A grammar is modest to the extent that by describing conditions and collisions of knowledge it can only provide questions concerning conceptual relations between fundamentally discrete language communities. It offers neither an agenda for interpretation nor a creeping resolution of problems; it functions only at the register of how meaning might be made without recourse to leaps associated with the urge to interpret; it is not meaning itself.

96. In Toshi Yoshida's woodcut *Imagination,* two forms face each other within an aura of pale yellow that bursts at the edges into flame. One form, composed of intricate stripes, towers over the other, a solid black lozenge; each is of a lightness and fluidity that defies its dense surface in part because of the precarious relationship one has to the other. These forms poise uncomfortably, as if about to tumble out of the frame and into one's lap. The dark form, subsumed in the flux of the lighter, larger companion, offers a huge maw facing the lozenge, a mouth about to bite. A commentary refers to the woodcut as a "dialogue of the inner imagination." The commentary, the above evocation of the woodcut, and its "vertiginous" effect on one viewer are shot through with a yearning for drama that may be meaningful in itself but whose techniques, if carried to possible conclusions, would indicate little more than the poetic urge of metaphysical meaning. Grammar would trace that yearning and perhaps not preserve it. On a table near the Yoshida a book by Adorno lies open and a statement, thinly underlined in pencil,

suggests a fleet reading of the relationship between woodcut, commentary, evocation, and the function of a grammar: "Theory cannot prolong the moment its critique depended upon." This new collision, generating a sense of extremis in the "introverted thought architect" (Adorno), forges neither a private beginning nor a public end but is, grammatically, a condition of analysis.

97. The final canvas is divided in such a way that readers of Pollock's painting can view it as entertaining a circle, from the first known self-portrait (at nineteen years of age) to the dripped strokes of the revolutionary "Action" period. The last work not only suggests a circular career—in that perhaps a cul-de-sac—but embraces the myth of Pollock already fashioned by his audience. At once the reliable signature of opulent and layered line, and at the same time a sudden return to portraiture undiscoverable elsewhere—the signs of his doubt presumably embodied in the fact that the face, an aged version of the first work, is half abstracted, in process of erasure as it points toward the left panel, the sign of Pollock's labor if not legend. The final painting is taken to be retrograde, indicative of the frustration and failure dogging his last years. Rather than a partial solution to an impasse, and not perceived as even an exercise in that direction, the final canvas is viewed as Pollock's "total collapse." As collapse, both panels reverberate with nostalgia, while the smallness of the work points to a failure to envision his own demise on a grand scale. It is the smallest painting of Pollock's maturity and more anecdotal of his life than of his art (no *summa aesthetica*), as if the reduced abstraction must be not merely a pallid imitation of himself but something resurrected from adolescence. As an "explanation" of his life the painting succeeds, but only if the life concludes so that the work acquires the status of being the last without being a culmination, unlike van Gogh's *Crows over a Wheatfield,* which is read as no longer the crisis but its apotheosis, its catharsis. In Pollock's case, the lock to this key is less the complete works than the concept and performance of doubt underlying all his thickening painting. By his method of either cutting off or indeed lengthening paintings he could articulate enough skepticism of the moment with enough confidence that

the statement of doubt would be unmistakable. Neither liked nor disliked, but unmistakable. If anything, the last painting dramatizes doubt too substantively, too theatrically; at last the ego is deliberately inscribed in the work. But the relations between the dissolving face and the abstract panel are reminiscent of the "self-portrait" statement in Vermeer's *Allegory of Painting,* in which the face is known only by a death mask obliquely seen on the table beside the embodiment of Clio, muse of History—in effect, an ego at once present and not, a mirror doubled. The repetition of the former self, in Pollock's case, is itself repeated in the aura of doubt that marks the painting itself: the painting as ego statement doubting the efficacy of the ego enacting and enacted in it. Is this the spiral we see in the eyes of the final self-portrait, and that which introduces the movement toward and of the abstract panel? Doubt doubly dramatized; doubt itself doubled, even doubted (" − − P = P"). In that sense we have two doubtful selves doubting each other by their proximity, and also by their proximity doubting the trained reader of previous Pollocks, who in his or her doubt in the face of the last face would find a strategy, not unlike Pollock's, for drawing the line.

98. "And gags for skool and crossbuns and whopes he'll enjoyimsolff over our drawings on the line!" (*Finnegans Wake,* 308)

Selected Bibliography

Adorno, Theodor. *Prisms.* Trans. Samuel and Shierry Weber. London: Neville Spearman, 1967.

Arnold, V. I. *Catastrophe Theory.* Trans. G. S. Wassermann. New York: Springer-Verlag, 1986.

Benjamin, Walter. *Illuminations.* Trans. Harry Zohn. New York: Schocken, 1969.

———. *Origin of German Tragic Drama.* Trans. J. Osborne. London: New Left Books, 1977.

Blanchot, Maurice. *The Gaze of Orpheus.* Trans. Lydia Davis. Barrytown, N.Y.: Station Hill, 1981.

Danto, Arthur. *Transfiguration of the Commonplace.* Harvard: Harvard University Press, 1981

Derrida, Jacques. *Dissemination.* Trans. Barbara Johnson. Chicago: University of Chicago, 1981.

Eco, Umberto. *The Open Work.* Trans. Anna Cancogni. Harvard: Harvard University Press, 1989.

Frank, Elizabeth. *Pollock.* New York: Abbeville Press, 1983.

Jakobson, Roman. *The Framework of Language.* Ann Arbor: Michigan Studies in the Humanities, 1980.

Joyce, James. *Finnegans Wake.* New York: Viking, 1939.

Kuspit, Donald B. "To Interpret or Not to Interpret Jackson Pollock." *Arts Magazine* 53 (March 1979): 125–27.

Lacan, Jacques. *Écrits: A Selection.* Trans. Alan Sheridan. New York: Norton, 1977.

———. *Encore: Le Seminaire de Jacques Lacan,* vol. 10. Paris: Seuil, 1975.

———. *Four Fundamental Concepts of Psychoanalysis.* Trans. Alan Sheridan. New York: Norton, 1978.

Landau, Ellen G. *Jackson Pollock.* New York: Harry N. Abrams, 1989.

Lyotard, J.-F. *The Differend: Phrases in Dispute.* Trans. Georges Van Den Abbeele. Minneapolis: University of Minnesota Press, 1988.

Marin, Louis. *Détruire La Peinture.* Paris: Editions Galilée, 1977.

Preziosi, Donald. *Rethinking Art History.* New Haven: Yale, 1989.

Rubin, William. "Jackson Pollock and the Modern Tradition." *Artforum* 5 (February–March 1967): 28–37, (April–May 1967): 18–31.

Thom, René. *Structural Stability and Morphogenesis.* Reading, Mass.: W. A. Benjamin, 1975.

Wildgen, Wolfgang. *Catastrophe Theoretic Semantics.* Philadelphia: John Benjamins, 1982

Wittgenstein, L. *Culture and Value.* Trans. Peter Winch. London: Basil Blackwell, 1980.

———. *A Philosophical Grammar.* Trans. Anthony Kenny. London: Basil Blackwell, 1974.

———. *Philosophical Investigations.* Trans. G.E.M. Anscombe. London: Basil Blackwell, 1958.

———. *Remarks on Colour.* Trans. Linda M. McAlister and Margarete Schattle. Berkeley and Los Angeles: University of California Press, 1978.

———. *Remarks on the Philosophy of Psychology.* Trans. G.E.M. Anscombe. London: Basil Blackwell, 1980.

———. *Tractatus Logico-Philosophicus.* Trans. C. K. Ogden. London: Routledge and Kegan Paul, 1922.